FIGHTING
IN HOCKEY

FIGHTING
IN HOCKEY

J. Alexander Poulton

OVER
TIME
BOOKS

The Publisher: OverTime Books is an imprint of Éditions de la Montagne Verte

Library and Archives Canada Cataloguing in Publication

Poulton, J. Alexander (Jay Alexander), 1977–

   Fighting in hockey / J. Alexander Poulton.

Includes bibliographical references.

ISBN 978-1-897277-75-1

   1. National Hockey League—History. 2. Violence in sports. 3. Hockey. I. Title.

GV847.8.N3P685 2012   796.962'64   C2012-907090-4

Project Director: Deanna Howell
Editor: Kathy van Denderen
Cover Images: Front: © Radius Images / Corbis and © Photos.com; back: © Photos.com

We acknowledge the financial support of the Government of Canada through the Canada Book Fund (CBF) for our publishing activities.

 Canadian   Patrimoine
Heritage   canadien

PC: 1

Contents

Introduction 7

Chapter 1
**A Short History of Fighting and the Role
of the Enforcer** 13

Chapter 2
A Divisive Subject 34

Chapter 3
The Code 59

Chapter 4
The Greatest Fighters in NHL History 70

Chapter 5
There Is No "I" in Team 174

Chapter 6
The Ugly Side of Hockey 209

Chapter 7
**Tail of the Tape: Fighting Facts,
Stats and Quotes** 234

Chapter 8
The Lighter Side of Fighting 243

Chapter 9
Final Words 255

Fighting in Hockey: A Timeline 259

List of Fighting Terms 265

Notes on Sources 267

Dedication

To my wife

Introduction

*It's not the size of the dog in the fight, it's the
size of the fight in the dog.*

–Mark Twain

Hockey is a physical sport. That above all is
understood by everyone involved in the
game and by the fans cheering on their favorite
team. The mere act of putting large athletes on
the ice strapped onto razor-sharp blades, wearing
a suit of armor and traveling at high velocities
almost guarantees that eventually two of these
behemoths are going to collide. Fans expect that
level of aggression, and the National Hockey
League promotes it. Looking into the professional
history of the game, hockey has always been
a rough-and-tumble sport, but opinions differ on
the nature of the game in its more violent
byproduct: the infamous hockey fight.

Fighting in an NHL game is officially against the rules, but since organized hockey began, it has always been a part of the game. Many would argue that the game has remained so popular and has brought in new fans solely because of fighting. Increasingly, however, more people are calling for a moratorium on fighting in hockey. With the recent deaths in the last five years of pugilists Bob Probert, Derek Boogaard, Wade Belak and Rick Rypien, the calls for an end to the violence on the ice are beginning to be heard in the head office of the NHL. Before coming to any conclusions on the matter, a little perspective might be in order.

The job of a tough guy, goon, enforcer, policeman or whatever you want to call these types of players, is one of the hardest in all sports. These players must go out on the ice every game knowing that they run the risk of being punched in the face, getting hurt or even hurting another player. But the guys do it, and a lot of them are willing to take these risks. They believe that the code of the fighter—the set of unwritten rules rarely spoken of—is enough to guide a path through all dangers of the game, as long as the other players follow the same rules.

As the game has evolved, the role of fighting has changed little. From hockey's inception, players have fought each other. It's the nature of a contact sport; however, something sets hockey apart from other sports such as football or baseball. Sometime in the past, fighting entered into the culture of the sport, and there it has remained.

You will see in reading this book that without fighting, hockey might not exist today, and that North Americans could all be playing soccer instead. Fighting between players brought people to NHL games when the league had just five teams and teetered on the edge of failure during the Depression years. Hockey was promoted as a violent sport, and the fans came out in droves to watch the games. The fans' love of the more bloodthirsty aspects of the game explains the popularity of players like Eddie Shore, whom some fans loved and others loved to hate. Every time the Boston Bruins played in a new city, the arena was packed with people waiting to see what Shore would do next. The NHL has capitalized brilliantly on its growing popularity and used fighting to grow its brand.

But is the violence in hockey becoming too much? If you take some time to review the arguments from those who want to keep fighting in the game and those who want it out, you'll see that both sides make valid points. Where do you stand? Once you know the history and the code that hockey players live by, you might see the future of the game differently.

Whatever side you may fall on, the job and role these players have had in the history of the game has been great. Players like the original tough guy Sprague Cleghorn, who was known as the meanest son-of-a-gun on the ice, had general managers in the league calling for his permanent expulsion from the NHL. Then came the NHL expansion in 1967 to 12 teams and with it a dilution of the talent pool. The effect was a league looking to bring more fans into its stands and teams with less talent relying on physical force to win games. The expansion gave birth to the dreaded 1970s incarnation of the Philadelphia Flyers—aptly named "Broad Street Bullies"—whose intimidation tactics allowed them to bully their way to two Stanley Cups and change the game forever.

The Broad Street Bullies gave rise to a new breed of hockey players known as "enforcers," whose sole job was to protect the star players on their team, and the 1980s was the golden decade of the enforcer. Players like Bob Probert, Dave Semenko and Tiger Williams ruled the ice with an iron fist, creating room for players like Steve Yzerman and Wayne Gretzky. Consequently, that decade saw the most prolific scoring ever, with Mario Lemieux and the Great One reaching plateaus once thought impossible. Back in the 1980s, fights were just fights—you know, the old hockey adage of "boys will be boys." But things started to change. Both the Good Friday Massacre, a brawl between the Quebec Nordiques and the Montreal Canadiens in 1984, and the Punch-up in Piestany in 1987 brought fighting in hockey into a whole new phase. The public began to see that fighting was no longer spontaneous, done in the heat of the moment—it was beginning to look like scripted violence. And it would only get worse.

The McSorley incident in 2000 showed an ugly side of hockey in a visceral way as never seen before. Almost four years later to the day, in a game between the Vancouver Canucks and the Colorado Avalanche, Canucks forward Todd Bertuzzi sought revenge on Avs forward Steve Moore.

In both incidents, TV viewers at home and fans at the games saw the injured player suffering on the ice, and the level of the violence shocked them. Hockey was becoming a gladiator sport, and by the looks of the violence on the ice, someone was going to die. The NHL said it was going to change, and the league got tougher on players for infractions and for fighting, but in the end, the league still has problems.

This was never more apparent as in the deaths of Wade Belak, Rick Rypien and Derek Boogaard, all of whom were fighters that battled drug and alcohol addiction and depression. After their deaths, it was revealed, in the case of Boogaard, that he had been suffering from chronic traumatic encephalopathy, a brain disease brought on by repeated blows to the head.

Although the question about what to do about fighting in hockey is difficult to answer, there are ways to address the issues and not simply revert to old sayings and nostalgia for a type of hockey that has long since gone. Fighting in hockey is a controversial topic at all levels of the game, but the conversation needs to continue in order to keep the game safe and enjoyable for generations to come.

Chapter 1

A Short History of Fighting and the Role of the Enforcer

We know that hockey is where we live, where we can best meet and overcome pain and wrong and death. Life is just a place where we spend time between games.

–Fred Shero

Fighting has been part of hockey since the sport's birth. Some of the earliest newspaper reports from around the late 1800s about the emerging sport tell of brutal fights between players, between players and officials, between players and fans and even between players and figure skaters. The inclusion of fighting in hockey goes deep into the cultural and historical past of North America. This aspect of the game was not something that was simply inserted to make hockey more entertaining or to sell more tickets—fighting in hockey says something about our past, about our culture and about who we are as fans.

The history of fighting and the history of hockey go hand in hand. Hockey developed out of several games played by Scottish and Irish immigrants and Native people in Nova Scotia. Those games, like shinty from Scotland, hurling from Ireland and *baggataway* from the Mi'kmaq people, are all precursors to hockey and all known for a certain level of violence. As those games changed and adapted to life in the Great White North, their violent aspects were integrated into the new game called hockey.

The people who played the sport in its early beginnings were not exactly from the highest economic class. Nova Scotia was primarily a military port around the late 1700s and early 1800s, and when the soldiers had some time off in the winter, they would play the sports they loved. The soldiers, being young men with nothing to do, would not play nice all the time, and sometimes fights broke out in these "friendly" games. As hockey became more organized, rivalries developed between teams, towns and villages and between the social classes. Even with the development of a system of rules and regulations, violence in the game still persisted.

By the late 1800s, hockey was already entrenched into Canadian culture from coast to coast. Leagues began to sprout up, and by 1893, Lord Stanley, the Governor General of Canada, donated his Dominion Cup to hockey, giving all teams a chance at the sport's top prize. Naturally, rivalries were quickly born, and out of that came intense, physical and sometimes violent hockey games. There were fights, high sticks and vicious checks in every game, but on occasion some of these competitions got out of hand.

One of the most intense leagues in those early days of hockey was the Federal Amateur Hockey League (FAHL). Founded in 1903, the FAHL was composed of teams from Ontario and Quebec. For its inaugural season, the league started with four teams, the Ottawa Capitals, the Montreal Wanderers, Montreal Le National and the Cornwall Hockey Club. Rivalries and bad blood were already established between Ottawa and Cornwall from previous seasons, but the addition of the Montreal Le National brought increased tension to games because they were the first all-francophone team to play in an all-anglo league.

By the 1906–07 FAHL season, the league had seen several teams come and go, and with them the rivalries would fade, but one rivalry between cities lasted for several years—Ottawa versus Cornwall. The two teams were not fond of each other, and since the clubs played so often during a season, the fans and players had plenty of time to develop a healthy hatred for one another. During that 1906–07 season, on a cold March night, the game between the Ottawa Victorias (who joined the FAHL for the 1905–06 season) and the Cornwall Hockey Club got way out of hand.

The animosity between the two teams could be felt before the first puck was dropped. Ottawa was the dominant team in the league that season and they had already handed Cornwall several embarrassing losses. This game was one of the teams' last meetings of the season, and Cornwall wanted to ensure the Victorias would not forget it. If Cornwall could not beat their opponents on the score sheet, they would beat them on the ice.

The game was quiet for the first half (games back then had two 30-minute halves), but by the second, several players on both sides began to take liberties on the ice and the tension quickly mounted. Cornwall forward Owen McCourt was the most physical of the players, and his main target that night was Ottawa's Arthur Throop. The battle between the two players was made worse because in those days, players did not change lines. One or two relief players might remain on the bench, but in general, a player stayed out on the ice for the entire game. This ensured that if any grudge between players needed to be resolved, someone would eventually get a chance.

The antagonism between McCourt and Throop reached its peak late in the second half when Throop took McCourt hard into the boards.

After McCourt shook off the hit, he skated directly for Throop with his stick raised above his shoulders, ready to take his opponent's head off. McCourt swung his stick down like an axe, hitting Throop above the eye and opening up a huge gash that sent a gush of blood across the ice. Both benches immediately emptied and a brawl ensued.

Ottawa forward Charles Masson made it his mission to get back at McCourt for what he had done to his teammate. Masson made his way through the tangled bodies, intent on retribution. Masson found McCourt in the brawl, raised his stick above his head and swung down with all his might. The stick struck McCourt's unprotected head right on the temple and sent him crashing to the ice. With revenge handed out, Masson then rejoined the brawl, leaving McCourt in a bloodied pile. It wasn't until the referees got everything under control that they realized McCourt was still lying on the ice and not moving.

Cornwall players rushed to his side. McCourt eventually regained consciousness and was carried off. To everyone's surprise, McCourt made his way back out onto the ice but only played five more minutes before retiring to the dressing room, complaining of dizziness and confusion. Once the game had ended, the team's medic knew something was wrong with McCourt and he was rushed to the hospital. On the way there,

McCourt passed out and never woke up. He died two days later in hospital from a severe brain hemorrhage caused by the blow to his head.

The news of McCourt's death was a great shock to the hockey world, especially since he had continued to play after being hit on the head. People were searching for answers and someone to blame, and in the end, police issued a warrant charging Charles Masson with McCourt's death.

In the ensuing trial, Masson's defense lawyer argued that McCourt had received several knocks to the head during the course of the game, so it could not be said with certainty that the blow delivered by Masson led to McCourt's death. Because of the lack of evidence, Masson was acquitted of all charges and set free.

This event is an extreme case of fighting in hockey and was the result of a tolerant attitude toward violence that was becoming an inherent part of the game. It was also an aspect of the game that was promoted and codified in the rulebook with the formation of the National Hockey League in 1917. In 1918, the NHL introduced the two blue lines, and with that came the advent of forward passing, though only in the neutral zone. The introduction of the lines changed the nature of the game, meaning that the neutral zone became the most violent area of the ice where one team would try to speed through while the other put up a roadblock and used any means necessary to stop the other team. This naturally led to more fights, and buckets of blood spilled on the ice. The NHL had the power to put a complete stop to fighting in the sport by taking a firm stand, but in 1922 the league chose to keep it as a part of the game. That year, the NHL brought in Rule 56, which regulated fighting, or fisticuffs as they called it, giving the fighters a five-minute penalty rather than ejecting them from the game. It was clear to the league and to the team owners that if the NHL and its teams were to have a future, fighting would have to be part of it.

Fighting was not only tolerated by the league but was also used heavily in the promotion of the NHL, and no one was better at that than promoter Tex Rickard. After noticing the success of the New York Americans, who joined the NHL in 1925, Rickard thought he could capitalize on developing a rival in New York, and in 1926, he founded the New York Rangers. Hockey was not an instant hit with New Yorkers, but using his experience as a boxing promoter, Rickard knew which aspects of hockey to focus on to get fans into Madison Square Garden. Before a game night, Rickard hired ambulances to blare their sirens through the streets of Manhattan on their way toward Madison Square Garden, luring out the curious to see what all the commotion was about. While the fans waited to get into the Garden, Rickard instructed the ambulances to park in front of the building and pretend to wait for the bloodied and battered players who were expected to flow out of the arena once the game began.

In the games against the Boston Bruins in the late 1920s and '30s, Rickard played a masterstroke of marketing by blanketing the city with "WANTED: DEAD OR ALIVE" posters of the Bruins' most hated and violent villain, Eddie "Old Blood and Guts" Shore. Fans showed up in droves to boo the "evil" Eddie Shore. The marketing worked. The New York Rangers became firmly entrenched in the NHL throughout the Depression while other teams folded operations during those hard times. Hockey survived, and during World War II, the game won the hearts of spectators. People needed a distraction from the realities of war, and hockey's fast and physical game brought out the fans.

Coach Jack Adams

Hockey is a high-octane game that stirs up strong emotions—emotions that can sometimes get the better of those behind the bench. As a player, Jack Adams was tough and physical on the ice, but he could also score a few goals. Adams turned pro in 1917, joining the Toronto Arenas. He also played with the Vancouver Millionaires of

the Pacific Coast Hockey Association, then
returned to the NHL with the Toronto St. Pats
and the Ottawa Senators before hanging up his
skates in 1927.

Adams suffered his fair share of injuries in his
days on the ice, but hockey players were "real
men" in those days and they dealt with their
injuries in a manner appropriate to the time.
"When you got cut in those days, you skated to
the boards and the trainer sloshed off the blood
with a sponge he kept in a bucket. Then he
patched you up with a slice of adhesive tape,"
described Adams. For Adams, though, that fighting hockey spirit never left his soul; he carried it
over into his 20-year coaching career behind the
bench for the Detroit Red Wings.

Adams was as fiery on the ice as he was off,
regularly getting into shouting matches with referees over perceived injustices to his team, much
to the delight of fans and his team. However,
nothing tops one episode during the 1942 Stanley Cup finals when Adams' Detroit Red Wings,
up three games to none over the Toronto Maple
Leafs, tried to close out the series with a game-
four victory. Throughout the first three games of
the series, Adams mocked the Leafs' effort in the
games, and in his mind, the Red Wings had
the series wrapped up. "We out-fought them,
out-hustled them and should have beat them

7–3," he said after a 4–2 win in game two. Despite being down by three games, though, the Leafs were not about to give up, and in game four, they came back fighting.

Game four started badly for the Leafs, who were down by two goals at the midway point of the second period. It was time for desperation hockey and a little luck. By the end of the second period, the Leafs managed to pot two goals to tie up the game. The Red Wings came back swinging in the third period and scored the go-ahead goal. That lead did not last long. Two goals from Toronto's Syl Apps and Nick Metz put the Leafs ahead for the first time in the game by a score of 4–3.

As if the close score wasn't enough entertainment for the fans, during a pause in play, with just two minutes remaining in the game, the Red Wings Eddie Wares directed a volley of verbal abuse at referee Mel Hardwood. Wares was still fuming over what he perceived as the referee's bias against the Wings, who had received a disparate number of penalties throughout the course of the game. When Wares refused to leave the ice and continued his verbal assault, Harwood gave him a 10-minute misconduct.

Moments after the play resumed, Harwood spotted Detroit with too many men on the ice and whistled the play dead to assess the infraction. Red Wings forward Don Grosso was called out to

serve the two-minute penalty, and he gave Harwood a piece of his mind on his way across the
ice. But Grosso wasn't done. He skated right up to
Harwood, dropped his stick and gloves and challenged the referee to a fight. Harwood would have
none of it and gave Grosso another 10-minute
misconduct for abuse of officials. When calm was
restored, the game ended with the Leafs winning
by a score of 4–3. But the entertainment that
night was far from over.

As Harwood was working out the final penalty
count with the other off-ice officials, Detroit
coach Jack Adams was in a fury over the penalties handed out to his team. But instead of filing
an official grievance with the league, Adams
jumped onto the ice and headed straight for Harwood. The portly but surprisingly agile head
coach pounced on the unsuspecting referee and
started raining blows down on his head. While
Harwood and Adams traded haymakers in the
penalty box, Detroit fans followed Adams' lead
and began attacking the linesmen. The growing
mob almost reached league president Frank
Calder, but police officers whisked him away
before the crowd had a chance to vent their
anger. Adams, for his attack on the referee, was
fined by the league and suspended from attending the rest of the playoffs. Living up to his fiery
reputation, Adams refused to go without a fight.

"They can't keep me out of Maple Leaf Gardens. I'll buy my way into the place!" Adams defiantly uttered to reporters before the start of game five in Toronto.

The Leafs used the momentum from game four to win the next three games and take the Stanley Cup, becoming the only team in NHL history to ever come back from a 3–0 series deficit. Adams begrudgingly accepted his fate.

The Expansion

The NHL became more popular than ever around the time of Jack Adams and Eddie Shore, and the league would only continue to increase its audience. Even though fights and bloodied noses were still part of the game, the era of the Original Six was probably the most gentlemanly in NHL history. It was an era when the code of conduct on the ice ruled. The 1950s and '60s were relatively calm times for the league, with no major incidents to scar its image, but after the 1967 expansion to 12 teams, the face of the league changed.

The expansion was necessary for the NHL to survive the competition from other professional sports, but the sudden opening up of jobs meant that the pool of talent from which to choose suddenly became a lot thinner. Less skill to choose from meant tougher, bigger players entered the league, and as a result, violence on the ice increased.

Suddenly, the league had a place for guys like Eddie Shack, Wayne Maki, Dave Schultz and a host of other players who would never have made it into the NHL back in the days of the Original Six. With players better known for their physical prowess than their hockey talents, violent incidents on the ice increased tenfold.

On January 13, 1968, in a game between the expansion Oakland Seals and the Minnesota North Stars, Stars forward Bill Masterton was carrying the puck into the Seals zone when the Seals Larry Cahan and Ron Harris checked him hard into the boards. The impact caused Masterton to lose his balance, and he fell backwards, smashing his unprotected head on the ice. The force of the blow was so severe that it caused blood to spew from his nose and mouth. Masterton lost consciousness and never woke again. He died two days later in hospital at the age of 29. To this day, the sight of Masterton lying on the ice still haunts Harris.

"It bothers you the rest of your life. It wasn't dirty and it wasn't meant to happen that way. Still, it's very hard because I made the play. It's always in the back of my mind," said Harris in a 2003 interview.

Another incident during a preseason game on September 21, 1969, had people wondering if the NHL and the sport in general was on the right path. In that game, the St. Louis Blues Wayne Maki and the Boston Bruins "Terrible" Ted Green started in on each other with a few hard hits, but the two tough players quickly escalated the affair. The hits turned into cross checks followed by a flurry of slashes and spears before Maki lost his temper and swung his stick at Green's head, severely fracturing his skull.

Green nearly died as a result of the injury; he needed three surgeries and a steel plate in his head just to repair the damage. He missed the rest of the season but eventually returned to hockey, finishing his career in the World Hockey Association. Both Maki and Green were charged by police for assault and were later acquitted. This was the first time in the history of the NHL that a player was charged for a crime that occurred during a game.

The face of the game took a new turn when the Philadelphia Flyers made it their plan to get bigger and badder, adding players like Dave Schultz and Bobby Clarke, who went on to form the Broad Street Bullies. The Flyers fought and intimidated their way to the top of the NHL, winning back-to-back Stanley Cups in 1974 and 1975. In the past, teams had just one or two opposing physical players they had worry about, but the Flyers made the physical game a team philosophy—their leading scorer Bobby Clarke was one of the worst offenders, taking every opportunity to hack and slash players at will.

"If we can, we'll intimidate our rivals. We try to soften them up, then pounce on them. There are lots of ways to play this game. Our way works," said Flyers head coach Fred Shero about the team's approach to the game.

The Flyers had only a handful of real fighters, but the entire team bought into Shero's premise of team toughness, so they found success. Other teams in the NHL tried to emulate or at least match the Flyers in toughness, and as a result, the 1970s was a decade filled with hockey blood.

The team philosophy of the Flyers eventually died out, but the tough guys who could fight better than they played hockey remained in the league, ushering in the era of the super enforcer. Guys like Dave "Tiger" Williams, Chris Nilan, Bob Probert and Dave Semenko found a role as the protectors of the stars in their clubs. They were the new intimidation factor in the NHL, and if they did their jobs well, they retained a spot on their teams.

This new breed of tough guy was in the league for one reason and one reason only—to fight. If he scored a few goals, great, but the enforcer's primary job was to protect stars like Wayne Gretzky, and that was it. The league was now filled with hockey players who had only one function in the club—the fighter, the grinder, the scorer or the defender. In the earlier decades of the NHL, players had to be the complete player, fighting their own fights and defending their territory when needed, but coaches now had a lineup of role-specific players to put out on even strength, power plays and penalty kills. The increasing number of teams required coaches to fit players into specific niches on the ice, and the fighter occupied an important role.

For the enforcer, the 1980s were the golden years. Most teams had enforcers, and they happily abided by their warrior code. As a result, the superstars thrived, giving birth to a decade of goal scoring led by Gretzky and Lemieux. But it was not a peaceful decade by any means; the price for all that room on the ice was paid for in blood by the league's tough guys.

The NHL had tried ruling out brawls with the 1971 "third man in" rule, which stated that the first person to join a fight already in progress is automatically thrown out of the game. But by the early 1990s, with the league's 75th anniversary coming up in 1993, the NHL wanted to get away from the reputation of violence in the game, and so installed the Instigator Rule (Rule 56), which gave an extra two-minute penalty to the person who started the fight.

Neither rule did much to end fighting, but the rules did affect the team brawling that once marred the league. Before the installation of the instigator rule, the enforcer governed the ice, meting out justice according to the code. If a player went after a star, the enforcer would approach him and maybe warn him not to do it again or face the consequences. If the opposing player did not heed the warning, he and the enforcer would fight, or the enforcer would seek revenge on the other team's star player.

The instigator rule was a controversial rule in fighting because it led to the development of the staged fight, which the NHL doesn't like. With the instigator rule, both teams want to avoid getting that extra two-minute penalty, so what happens is that two players come out on the ice and mutually agree to drop their gloves at the same time, thus avoiding the extra penalty. From the moment the rule was brought in, hockey purists have hated it.

The league claimed that policing of the game belonged in the hands of the officials and not the enforcers. If things got out of hand on the ice, it was up to the league to dole out punishment within the confines of the NHL rulebook. Once the rule was enforced, the NHL noticed that fights did indeed drop for the 1992–93 season.

Many people opposed the instigator rule. The league was now controlling the ice, and players began to see that the executives did not have the courage to stand by their convictions and hand out appropriate fines and suspensions for on-ice incidents. The rule effectively handcuffed the enforcer from dishing out his own fines and penalties on disrespectful players. The rule took away the spontaneity of fighting and cheapened the enforcer's role; his power to effect peace on the ice was removed, and as a result, players who played dirty began to rule the league. Fighting may have been reduced, but there was an increase in stick work and knee-on-knee hits as well as the infamous head shots that have taken out some of the best players of the game and forced many into early retirement.

Without the fear of an enforcer to answer to, these kinds of dirty hits have begun to plague the league, even taking out the new superstar Sidney Crosby who received his first concussion on January 1, 2011, during the NHL Winter Classic when Crosby's Penguins played the Washington Capitals. On an innocent-looking play, when Crosby did not even have the puck, the Capitals Dave Steckel blindsided Crosby with an elbow to the head, knocking him to the ice. Steckel received no suspensions or fines for his actions and later claimed that the hit was an accident;

however, video of the incident leaves little doubt that he fully intended to smack Crosby. Without fear of retribution, players of Steckel's caliber will continue to take runs at the league superstars to take them out of the game.

The new fighting rules have also affected the enforcer's profession. Rather than taking away the revenge aspect to the game that many people complained about before the rules were enacted, headhunters was brought into the league. Players like Matt Cooke and Brad Marchment became standard hunters, taking out players with a shot to the knees or to the head. And so the enforcer is handicapped under the instigator rule because he is not able to drop the gloves and challenge offending players without risking the additional penalty. Even though the league has had countless opportunities to rid the league of cheap-shot players, on more than one occasion, a hit to the knee or a concussive head shot has not even garnered a two-minute penalty.

Since the outbreak of cheap hits and concussions, a movement has been on the rise to remove the instigator rule and let the players police themselves; it is a call for the return of the glory days of the NHL enforcer.

"I think the instigator has really diminished the level of respect players have for one another nowadays," said retired enforcer Rob Ray, in

Bernstein's book *The Code*. "It prevents players from policing themselves and handling their own affairs in a way that forces everyone to be accountable. Once that rule went into place, that is when the game got a lot more violent in my opinion.... The cheap shots, the high sticks, the dirty play, and the overall lack of respect are all byproducts of that stupid rule in my eyes.... Other than the rare fine or suspension handed down by the league, there is no recourse for players playing dirty and getting away with it."

Player injuries increased after the 2004–05 lockout when certain rule changes were put in place to make the game faster. With the removal of the red line and the hindering of the goaltenders ability to play the puck, the number of injuries skyrocketed because of players taking liberties. Suddenly you had players speeding through the neutral zone at top speeds going into their opponent's zone, making them vulnerable targets. With the rule changes, general managers also turned away from picking many of the tough guys for their teams, instead they chose faster more offense-minded players. The result was many smaller players taking liberties on the ice and a sickening increase in head injuries, with the offending players having no one to answer to except the league.

When Pittsburgh Penguins Matt Cooke clearly targeted Boston Bruins Marc Savard's head on March 7, 2010, Cooke was penalized, even though the resulting injury effectively put an end to Savard's promising career. Consider also the Philadelphia Flyers Mike Richard's shoulder hit to the head on the Florida Panthers David Booth that occurred on October 24, 2009. Richards was ejected from the game but was not suspended by the league disciplinarian. Proponents of fighting point to incidents like these as clear examples of how enforcers are needed in the game to reduce injuries that often lead to more dire outcomes.

As people began to reevaluate the role of enforcers and their potential to root out cheap hits, the future of the policeman in the league was put into further doubt with the tragic deaths of Bob Probert, Rick Rypien, Derek Boogaard and Wade Belak.

All four players made their careers with their fists in the new NHL and did so willingly. They bought into the idea of their enforcer role because they had to if they wanted a job in the pros. Achieving their dreams came with a heavy price.

Since their deaths, the NHL promised to look into the issue of fighting in hockey more seriously, but the league has made these promises before and not much has changed.

Chapter 2

A Divisive Subject

> *By the age of 18, the average American has*
> *witnessed 200,000 acts of violence on televi-*
> *sion, most of them occurring during Game One*
> *of the NHL playoff series.*
>
> —Steve Rushin

Hockey by its very nature breeds physical play, but the game is unique in that it tolerates violence more than other professional sports do. It's why many hockey fans are attracted to the game—the fascination with violence—and hockey exploits this interest perfectly. Watch any game when two players drop their gloves, and every fan in the arena jumps up cheering wildly as the two gladiators throw punches.

As recently as the 2012 Stanley Cup playoffs, network viewing numbers indicated that the more contentious and violent the games, the more people tune in. The Philadelphia Flyers–Pittsburgh Penguins series in the playoffs were rife with hatred, violence and fighting, which gave both American and Canadian networks their highest ratings. Fans of all ages, both male and female, openly cheer when one of their players beats another up, and often, the bloodier the fight, the better.

Fighting is an aspect of the game that has been used to sell it to the fans for years, and the NHL and the team owners have been pushing it since 1917 when the league was first formed. The current boss of the NHL, Gary Bettman, said at a 2007 press conference: "Fighting has always had a role in the game...from a player safety standpoint, what happens in fighting is something we need to look at just as we need to look at hits to the head. But we're not looking to have a debate on whether fighting is good or bad or should be part of the game."

And NHL commissioner, Bettman knows better than anyone that if the physical edge was removed from the game, he would face a shrinking audience, upset advertisers and anger team owners. Even Bettman's former colleague, the man who once had the responsibility as the NHL chief disciplinarian, Colin Campbell (1998–2011) said in Adam Proteau's excellent book *Fighting the Good Fight*: "We sell hate. Our game sells hate."

Both Bettman and Campbell are correct in their statements that hockey has always been packed with fighting and violence, but removing any kind of purposeful physicality would alter the pace of the game. No longer could players deliver body checks to send a message. No longer would fighters roam the ice, and the players would be too careful and the game would slow to a crawl. Imagine football without the tackles; it wouldn't be the same sport, and so it would be with hockey. There are also legions of writers, hockey minds and fans who believe in the old adage, "If it ain't broke, don't fix it."

The Case for Fighting

Anybody who says they don't like fighting in the NHL have to be out of their minds.

–Don Cherry

Many people believe fighting in hockey is part of the game for a reason. Although it is impossible to say when the first fight occurred in hockey, accounts from the late 1800s of games between rival cities are rife with fighting and hard checks, and apart from a few dainty women fainting at the sight of blood, these games were popular and helped to spread the sport across North America. And the fighting attitude has served hockey well over the years, with Canada winning countless international medals and acting as the archetype for hockey that other nations aspire to.

In a fast-paced sport laced with physical play and high emotion, things are bound to get out of hand on occasion, and that's when players drop the gloves. Even with imposing regulations, penalties and fines, it is almost impossible to keep players from getting into scraps. Since the establishment of the professional game, the role of fighting has changed but is still essential. In the modern league with 30 teams, the distribution of the most talented players is not as even as it once was in the Original Six era of the NHL. So now, we have only a few great players on any one team if they are lucky. At the win-at-all-costs level of the NHL, if one of those talented players were to get injured, the team would be less effective and more likely to lose games. So this is where the enforcer or tough guy comes in. His job is to protect star players and keep the opposing players in line if any of them should get physical with the star.

Such was the role of Marty McSorley, who for years in Edmonton and then in Los Angeles was tasked with protecting the game's greatest player, Wayne Gretzky. Every time Gretzky stepped out onto the ice, he was considered a constant offensive threat, but rare was the occasion that any opposing player tried to check him too hard or injure him because skating just a few feet away was his bodyguard, Marty McSorley, who would drop his gloves and attack the moment anyone touched the Great One. This protection allowed Gretzky a little more room to perform his magic, and without McSorley or tough guy Dave Semenko at his side, Gretzky might not have had the same career that he did.

Fighting advocates such as Don Cherry argue that the violence in the NHL today and the sheer number of injuries is a direct result of the diminished role of the enforcer to police the dirty hits and cheap shots. Without a fighter on a team, opposing players do not give their competition any respect, and that's when the injuries occur.

A case in point is the Montreal Canadiens from about 2005 to 2011. Former general managers Bob Gainey and Pierre Gauthier built up a team that was fast, crafty and focused on skill. The closest player they had to a tough guy was forward Travis Moen, but with players like Brian Gionta, Mike Cammalleri, Tomas Plekanec and Scott Gomez (on average, all small players), other teams loved to play against Montreal because of the team's lack of physical presence on the ice. As a result, Montreal players began to fall victim to injuries. Canadiens forward Andre Markov was taken out on a hit by the Pittsburgh Penguins Matt Cooke, and when six-foot-nine Zdeno Chara of the Boston Bruins forced (others might say "guided") Canadiens forward Max Pacioretty into the lightly padded edge of the glass at the Bell Centre, and Pacioretty sustained a fractured vertebra and a severe concussion, the Canadiens bench had no one to respond to Chara's act. Because of such incidents, other teams called the Canadiens soft and easy to play against.

Another incident that illustrates the need for fighters on a team occurred at the beginning of the 2011–12 season in a game between the Boston Bruins and the Buffalo Sabres. Bruins forward Milan Lucic took a run at the Sabres star goaltender Ryan Miller and sent him out of the game with a concussion. Immediately after the play, no one on the Sabres team, which included a decent lineup of known tough guys like Paul Gaustad, stood up to Lucic and tried to make him answer for what he did to Miller. Gaustad commented on his team's lack of action after the game, which they lost 4–3: "I'm embarrassed that we didn't respond the way we should have." He added, "We didn't push back. There's no reason to be scared. We had to go after it, and we didn't."

Whether it was a result of that hit or not, the Sabres had a terrible first half of the year and even when Miller finally did return he too did not look like the goaltender of old either. Moments like that get into the heads of players and affect how they play. It wasn't until later in the season that the Sabres began to turn things around and make a push for the playoffs, unfortunately just missing out by a few points.

Another instance of how allowing fighters in a game can help a team came after a particularly physical game between the Carolina Hurricanes and the New York Rangers in 2006 where of one of the Carolina players suffered a broken nose. For the next game between the two teams, the Hurricanes called up an enforcer from their minor league affiliate, and then-captain Rod Brind'Amour noticed that after a few games, "teams weren't so willing to run our guys. If you have [an enforcer] on the bench, other teams know there's going to be some retribution."

If fighting was removed from the game, many supporters have said that hockey would be reduced to a game of cheap shots and under-handed tactics, with the main victims being the stars of the game. Supporters of fighting believe it's a way of policing the game and keeping the cheap-shot artists in line. Having Bob Probert or Georges Laraque patrolling the ice for your team is a good incentive to play the game fairly or risk having to deal with an enforcer. But being the protector or policeman is not the only role that an enforcer can play.

Tough guys can also provide a catalyst for their club when the team is down by a couple of goals in a game. The sight of a fighter winning a bout and the subsequent crowd reaction has often led to a turnaround in games. Coaches will often send out their fighters when down a by a goal or two to reignite the energy on their team.

In the 2012 NHL playoffs during the Ottawa Senators and New York Rangers series with the Senators up three games to two and leading game six in Ottawa 1–0 in the first period, Brandon Prust of the Rangers and Chris Neil of the Senators started a heated scrap. The fight came about because Neil had taken a run at Rangers star Brad Richards, and Prust had taken a run at Senators star Erik Karlsson. Neil got the better of Prust in the fight, which pumped up the crowd and his team, but it was the Rangers who took inspiration from the fight and came back to win the game and stay alive for a seventh game.

After the game, Brad Richards commented to CBC reporter Cassie Campbell, "Can't say enough about Brandon Prust stepping up, huge fight, changed the momentum of the game. We didn't want to let him down."

Win or lose, a fair fight between two players can change the momentum of a game. Those who have played the game know the bond between players, and watching another player put himself out on the line can provide a spark to his team. After all, players are people too, and

during a game, a team can be down on themselves and lose focus from their game plan.

The example of the fight between Prust and
Neil is just one of thousands over the years in the
NHL that have helped change the outcome of
a match. It's not just fights that can change the
course of a game but also an opportunistic body
check. If talented players such as Brad Richards
and others like him see a need for hockey to
remain a physical sport, then shouldn't fighting
be part of the game?

Fighters also offer an essential element to the
game that draws people to arenas. Fighting can
be entertaining to watch, and since professional
sport is a business, having a tough guy on your
team helps boost revenue. The players are well
aware of this fact, and plenty of them are prepared to suit up every game and drop their gloves
when their team needs them. Not many people
are ready to admit the advantage or accept this
part of the game, but fights bring in the fans, and
fans spend money, which is one of the strongest
arguments for why the NHL still allows fighting.

In the professional sports world, all the clubs
compete for the fans' attention, and watching
two players fight is a guilty pleasure that draws
more fans to the sport annually. And in business,
if one thing is certain, it's that money talks.

As much as people like to see Alexander Ovechkin score a goal while on his back or watch a beautiful end-to-end rush by Steven Stamkos, heavy hitting and fighting sells tickets. To speak in terms of hockey nostalgia, as a sport of youth and innocence that should be enjoyed for its grace and rhythm, is to forget about the reality of the game since its very beginnings. It can be argued that professional hockey expanded to such a degree through the decades because of the fans' attraction to the more violent aspects of hockey. Can an institution such as hockey suddenly alter the way the game is played? For well over 100 years, kids have seen and played the game a certain way. The physical game and fighting is engrained in hockey's culture. You see it in the way the NHL promotes itself, you see it in commercials, movies and literature. Fighting is woven into the fabric of hockey's identity and cannot be removed so easily by a minority of vocal opponents.

Player after player in the minors and in the NHL have gone on record to keep fighting in the game. The great Bobby Orr, who was not known for fighting, has weighed in on fighting in the modern game: "Hockey is a tough game. With all the talk and everything that's going on right now, it frightens me a little bit that we are giving our players an excuse not to hit. I just hope that we don't take that out of our game at the pro level."

Stanley Cup champion Milan Lucic of the Boston Bruins went so far as to speak out against Canadian Hockey League president David Branch in a *Vancouver Province* article on March 1, 2012, when Lucic heard that the league was considering a ban on fighting. "I think there will be more injuries because there'd be no fear of fighting. The game will become dirtier," said Lucic. "And, for myself, I don't think I could have made the NHL the way I did without it."

Lucic also maintained that fighting in the junior leagues, "kept me out of trouble because it's a way of getting my aggression out." Lucic and other pro-fighting advocates have also pointed out that the men involved in the fighting do it to keep their jobs and put food on the tables for their families, so people outside the game have no right to stop these honorable players for earning a living.

Lucic explains that fighting takes place between grown men in the NHL, and if younger players are not prepared for the reality of a Zdeno Chara or a Georges Laraque coming their way down the ice, then the league will be filled with a group of rookies ill equipped to play the game. Fighting does not take place among a bunch of kids, and therefore, professional players understand what happens every time the gloves hit the ice. Don Cherry loves to point out that most people calling for a ban on fighting in the NHL are usually writers or others who have never played or watched the game.

The main reason that writers and the public have become involved in the debate of fighting in hockey is because of the topic's overwhelming coverage in the news. Turn on the television, open a newspaper or search the Internet, and you'll find a blaring headline or full reports on fighting in hockey. There never was a public outcry 30 years ago like the one that exists today when an incident takes place in hockey. The perfect example of this 24-hour coverage was during the opening rounds of the 2012 NHL playoffs. Granted, there was a higher number of suspensions and fights, but playoff hockey has always been more physical than the regular season games.

The Pittsburgh–Philadelphia series in the opening round of the 2012 playoffs was one of the focal points of media scrutiny. The series was one of the most watched in the playoffs. The high-scoring, fast-paced and fight-filled games even saw Penguins star Sidney Crosby drop his gloves against the Flyers Claude Giroux. The series was a classic by hockey standards—two teams with a natural hatred for each other played the series with a higher level of physical intensity that generated great excitement among the fans.

But instead of the news media focusing on the exciting level of hockey between two heated rivals, they plastered the television and papers with images of fights and pictures of bloodstained ice. Anyone who has watched hockey for the past 20 years will know that everything that occurred in the Flyers–Penguins series has happened before, many times over.

In the 1980s playoff matchups between the Montreal Canadiens and the Quebec Nordiques, the hockey violence appears much worse than what the Flyers and Pens series offered. At that time, the level of outrage at the violence on the ice was quickly dismissed as just another hockey game where passions got out of hand. The same cannot be said of the Flyers/Penguins series, when the media focused on all the negative aspects and would not let the issue go. It came to such a point that traditional media outlets like CNN and CBC national news ran feature stories on the violence in the playoffs.

Another example of the media's twisting of the hockey world came when Raffi Torres of the Phoenix Coyotes hit Chicago Blackhawks forward Marian Hossa with a flying check during game three of the Conference quarter finals. Hossa was taken off the ice on a stretcher. He suffered a severe concussion and was forced to sit out the rest of the playoffs.

Torres was not penalized, but a day later, NHL disciplinarian Brendan Shanahan announced that Torres was suspended for 25 games. Much was made about the hit on Hossa in the media, but what is confusing is that about a decade earlier, similar hits by Devils defenseman Scott Stevens on Paul Kariya and Eric Lindros that resulted in both players receiving severe concussions were hailed in the media for their effectiveness and deemed legal hockey hits. If Stevens still played today, he would have been vilified by the media and likely suspended for his actions on the ice.

After the Torres hit on Hossa, the media exploded with articles and news stories about violence in hockey, showing the images of the Torres hit along with a litany of other selected moments that painted hockey in a bad light.

Soon after, politicians, including the Governor General of Canada, began talking about the violence in hockey, and others who did not watch hockey regularly called for a complete overhaul of the game.

If the physical aspect of the sport is removed, we will be left with a game that is played like the All-Star game—all skill but with players showing little heart or emotion. It's not a game many fans would want to see. Players' safety is important, but knee-jerk reactions to specific violent instances in hockey will not serve the game well.

The Case Against Fighting

Fighting for peace is like screwing for virginity.

–George Carlin

For all the pro-fighting pundits arguing to keep fighting in hockey, there is a growing number of people starting to speak out against it. A few former enforcers have spoken up about the uglier side of fighting in the NHL, considering the recent deaths of NHLers Rick Rypien, Wade Belak, Bob Probert and others. Despite the history and popularity of fighting, those looking to ban the practice have an ever-increasing number of examples and arguments supporting their cause. However, this task will not be an easy one as they are up against an entrenched hockey culture that believes fighting is necessary in a business that makes billions of dollars on promoting the more violent aspects of the game.

While proponents of keeping fighting in the game have the support of the NHL and a public generally in favor of maintaining the status quo when it comes to hockey, the anti-fighting lobby is beginning to gain traction. But the obstacles are many.

One of the biggest obstacles to change is the NHL itself. Fighting sells tickets, all kinds of NHL merchandise and television ad space. The NHL has always maintained that intentional violence will not be tolerated, but by never punishing repeat offenders the way it should, the league almost gives license for players to continue to behave badly. A recent example of the NHL's lack of consistency came during the 2010–11 season during two contentious games between the Pittsburgh Penguins and the New York Islanders. The first game was filled with fights but was also marked by the rarest of hockey spectacles and most exciting to some fans—the goalie fight.

Penguins goaltender Brent Johnson took on Islanders goaltender Rick Dipietro, and in the tussle, Dipietro, who had a history of concussions, was knocked to the ice by a powerful right hand to his jaw. Neither Johnson nor Dipietro received any punishment by the league, thereby setting up a tense atmosphere when the two teams met again nine days later. Islanders general manager Garth Snow was never one to shy away from a fight in his career and was more than willing to employ enforcers on his team when he deemed them necessary. During the rematch in which Johnson had to defend himself against the Islanders Michael Haley for what he did to Dipietro, another incident occurred that left many wondering about the level of violence in the game.

Islanders forward Trevor Gillies is in the NHL for only one reason, and it's not because he is a talented skater or a deft playmaker. He was called up by the Islanders because he is a fighter and a goon. The moment he got out onto the ice that night, he was looking for trouble. Gillies found his victim in Penguins forward Eric Tangradi. Skating clear across the ice directly toward a clueless Tangradi, Gillies elbowed him in the face and then proceeded to punch him repeatedly while he was down on the ice trying to cover up his face.

Once the linesmen got things under control and pushed Gillies off the ice toward the dressing room, Gillies then returned to the edge of the ice and taunted Tangradi while the team's trainer was looking after the forward. After the Bertuzzi–Moore incident of 2004, one might have hoped the NHL would have learned its lesson in handing out punishment for revenge-motivated violence, but all Gillies got for his attack was a nine-game suspension. The NHL always likes to say that it has the players' best interests at heart, but when incidents such as this one and many others go relatively unpunished, then the players will continue to fight.

Gary Bettman has often repeated the call for player accountability but in the same breath dismisses any major changes to the league's stance on fighting, using the most common argument that it has always been a part of the game. What Bettman has not taken into account is that the nature of fighting has changed. In the early days of hockey with limited jobs for players, the NHL was populated by players known more for their skill rather than their fists. Fights did occur, and some of them were indeed epic and insanely violent, but they were rare and were usually the result of two players simply losing their cool. No enforcers or goons patrolled the ice. When Maurice Richard was slashed or cross-checked, it was up to him to protect himself in a fight. Not many players tried to go up against Gordie Howe because they knew he could stand up against the toughest. However, as the NHL expanded and more jobs opened up, talent became more precious. To protect that talent, teams began to use tough players to act as on-ice police. Fighting no longer was a byproduct of a physical game but a product used to sell tickets to blood-thirsty fans.

Proponents of fighting love to say that it has always been part of the game and therefore should continue. And fighting is what many people come to see during NHL games; every fan stands up and cheers when a fight occurs. The argument is that if fighting is taken out, the NHL will lose fans. This opinion is a narrow-minded view of fans and is one of the reasons why people watch and enjoy hockey. But what of the 2010 Vancouver Olympics hockey tournament, which had no fighting or dirty checking?

Somewhere around 26 million Canadians watched the final gold medal game between Canada and the United States. The American fans watched the game with just as much interest, garnering the best television ratings for a hockey game since the 1980 Miracle on Ice. The reasons for such passion for the game of hockey are clear: all the games were hard fought, players did not shy away from checking, skill was on display, defense could comfortably jump up into the play and the games never felt slow. The tournament was the perfect exhibition of what the NHL could be if it wanted to change. Only a few minor penalties were given throughout the Olympic tournament with at most a four-minute penalty for high-sticking drawing blood.

The same can be said for the World Championships of Hockey and the Canada/World Cup. Fans love to see hockey in its purest form, where the most talented players are allowed to flourish, unencumbered by the darker side of modern NHL hockey. Fighting cheapens the sport and brings an undesirable element into the game that resembles wrestling or mixed martial arts rather than hockey.

A move away from the clutch-and-grab, physically violent North American game has been something people and even NHL players have been talking about since the late 1960s and

1970s, when North Americans began to see that the rest of the world was playing a different brand of hockey and was controlling the international competitions. When hockey first burst onto the international scene, Canada was the dominant force. In the first Olympic hockey tournaments from 1920 to 1952, Canada all but owned the gold medal. Games against Japan, Finland, Switzerland, France and Poland ended with an average of 13 goals for the Canadians to one goal—if they were lucky—for the other teams. It wasn't until the 1948 Olympics that the world began to catch up. The days of Canada winning games with scores of 14–0 were over. Canada's last gold medal in 1952 before their 50-year drought at the Olympic Games was almost lost to a much improved American squad, followed closely in the standings by the Swedes. (The championship that year was decided by the team with the most points at the end of an eight-game round between nine countries).

Four years later, in 1956, the Russians won the gold medal, then in 1960 it was the Americans, then the Russians again in 1964. The Canadian dominance in hockey was over, and their physical style of hockey was beginning to look barbaric in comparison. Canada was falling behind not only in the Olympics but also in the World Championships and even at the junior level.

Doubts began to creep into the minds of Canadian hockey fans, but they were quickly replaced with the rationalization that the Europeans might have defeated our best amateur teams, but if they played our best NHL players, Canada could rightly reclaim the title of greatest hockey nation. This desire to settle the score gave birth to the 1972 Summit Series—Canada's best against the Soviet Union's best.

The Canadians walked into the series with supreme confidence. They were the NHL stars confronting a group of unknown Russian hockey players. The assumption was that hockey had always been a Canadian game and that it was, by birthright, the best. The Canadians had Phil Esposito, Ken Dryden, Jena Ratelle, the Mahovlich brothers and many other recent Hockey Hall of Fame inductees, while the Soviets were a lineup of personality-lacking drones of the communist system. Underestimating the Soviets was Canada's biggest mistake. From the moment the puck dropped, the Soviets sped around the ice, playing a fast-paced, skills-based game.

Team Canada was caught flatfooted and ended up losing the opening game 7–3. The loss resulted in collective disbelief among Canadian hockey fans and throughout the hockey world. The Canadian players were surprised by the Russians' level of play, and Canadian fans were almost insulted that their best and brightest players could do nothing to stop these "backward communists." Stripped of their competitive spirit and national pride, the Canadian players could not help but admire the style displayed by the Soviet players.

Serge Savard, who played in the 1976 Super Series between the Montreal Canadiens and the Soviet Red Army Club, said to a *Montreal Gazette* reporter after the first game, which ended in a 3–3 tie, "I like the style the Russians play for many reasons. I like it because it can't help but improve the skills of a hockey player. For too long we've put violence into our game, fighting and hitting guys over the head with your stick because that's what the crowd wanted to see, or what we thought the crowd wanted to see."

Luckily, Team Canada pulled out a nail-biting win in the 1972 Summit Series, but in the Super Series in 1976, the Russians humbled the eight NHL teams they played, winning five of the eight games. Only the Philadelphia Flyers and the Buffalo Sabres were able to win their games. It is worth noting that during the Soviet–Flyers game in 1976, the Flyers Ed Van Impe delivered a vicious body check on the Soviets top player, Valeri Kharlamov, laying him out on the ice for several minutes. When the officials did not call a penalty on the play, the irate Soviet coach

Vsevolod Bobrov pulled his team off the ice in protest at the brutality the Flyers displayed. The Soviet coach was eventually talked into bringing his team back out, but the players did not put much effort into the remaining time, shying away from battles in the corner and paying the price in front of the net. The game ended with the Flyers winning 4–1. The Canadian style of hockey had won, but it wasn't a victory they could be proud of.

The Super Series of 1976 proved that the Russian brand of hockey was based on skill and fair play while the Canadian game resorted to a physical game to win. In the eight games played during the Super Series, the Russians won five, tied one and lost two.

Despite the proof over the years that fighting and cheap shots are not a necessary ingredient for success in hockey, the belief still permeates all levels of North American hockey that fighting must be kept to regulate the overall violence on the ice and protect the stars of the league from cheap-shot artists. The claim is that intimidation is a valuable component in any team's arsenal and is effective in winning hockey games. For example, if Sidney Crosby is scared to go up against a certain physical player then he will be less likely to score.

This way of thinking completely ignores the realities of the way hockey is played. Dirty players have and always will be in the NHL or in any league—fighting has not stopped players like Bryan Marchment or Matt Cooke from delivering illegal hits over and over again. Sure, they have had to answer to the resident enforcer on occasion, but when their five minutes is up in the box, they are right back out on the ice and looking for opportunities to seek revenge.

As long as the teams and the NHL see a place for players such as Marchment and Cooke, the "policemen" of the league can fight all they want, which will not change the dirty tactics played out on the ice. The policing of hockey should be left in the hands of the league. Players like Cooke and Marchment should have been handled harshly for their long list of career infractions, and this alone is the only way to deal with cheap shots. Fighting for peace is a ridiculous notion. It has done nothing to keep those players who skirt the edge of the rulebook out of the game. They might have to answer to a Laraque or a Probert, but the same players are back in the next game, and if you look at their history, they have learned absolutely nothing from those "enforcers."

When many of their arguments fail to persuade, proponents of fighting like to lay the blame on media for making a big deal out of nothing—that hockey has always been just fine and is only now under scrutiny because of the 24-hour sports news channels and the proliferation of information on the Internet. Although hockey coverage has expanded, the concerns the media has brought to light are not made less valid because of the blanket coverage.

The hard facts about fighting and violence in the game are there for everyone to see, and the deaths of Rick Rypien, Bob Probert and Wade Belak have made the consequences of fighting all the more poignant. The media is doing its job; the NHL is not. The league knows the physical risks the players face when it comes to fighting, yet they do nothing because they believe that violence sells hockey, and hockey, in the end, is big business.

The NHL needs a leader willing to take the risk of losing out on the money they believe fighting brings in and to make the tough decisions in order to remove the barbarism from a sport that, at its best, displays skill and superior athletic performance.

Chapter 3

The Code

The code to me is 100 percent about respect. It is about the respect the players have for the game; the respect the players have for their peers; the respect the players have for the Stanley Cup; the respect the players have for the players who played before them and paved the way; and the respect the players have for the history of the game.

—defenseman Willie Mitchell

The code is the unwritten set of rules that governs all levels of hockey. It is a warrior code not taught in hockey schools or overseen by NHL executives, but it is a silent set of rules deeply rooted into every kid who has ever watched a favorite player on television or has set foot on the ice for weekend hockey practice.

No one really talks about the code. It is something players take for granted; it is thought to be written into the genetics of every person who has ever played the game or watched as a fan. Although there is no written code for hockey players to follow, the meaning behind the term is possible to define.

Hockey is the only major sport to allow fighting, within reason, during the context of the game. In other sports such as baseball and basketball, when punch-ups do occur, they are usually simple shoving matches that the referees quickly break up. Fights rarely go beyond a wrestling match in these sports because the threat of fines, lengthy suspensions and possible injury are enough to deter the players from losing further control. Hockey is different.

Fighting is seen as an integral part of how the game is played. In the fastest team sport in the world that allows huge, powerful men to crash into each other at top speeds, gliding across ice on thin blades and wearing suits of armor, emotions are without a doubt going to get heated. It has always been assumed in hockey that letting players fight under the watchful eyes of the referees allows them to blow off steam, cool off in the penalty box and then continue on with the game. This thinking might not sound rational, but fighting in hockey has been accepted because it is believed there is a method to the madness.

Football is also a fast, hard-hitting sport where huge, athletic, testosterone-filled men crash into each other throughout an entire game, but fighting is strictly forbidden. While other sports have their own unwritten codes of conduct, the tolerance for fighting in hockey has precipitated the development of more complex and detailed rules of engagement for the sport.

It is not just fighting in the game that brought about the development of the rules but also the nature of the sport itself. In baseball or football, if a player wants to seek out vengeance on a particular player, he must wait for the exact right moment, one that might never come. In baseball and football, brawls are usually spontaneous as the players are not in each other's faces at regular intervals. In hockey on the other hand, you are guaranteed to see the target of your ire several more times during the game. If a player slashes you or hits your captain, you are guaranteed that the offending player will be out on the ice again within a few minutes. This constant threat and fear of violence has contributed to the rise of the code as well and is in all sports but is present on every shift in hockey.

The unwritten rules are rarely formally discussed, but kids as young as 12 will know the basic tenets of the code. Coaches teach the code to them, it is discussed in lockers rooms before and after games, and their dads teach them the code on backyard rinks on weekends. For example, kids are aware from a young age that you don't cross-check another player when his back is turned, and you do not interfere with the opposing goaltender. These rules could be thought of as "Code 101," but the true breadth of the code only really comes into play when fighting is placed in the mix. In pee wee or midget hockey, if a player crosses the line, he will not have to answer for his misdeeds by fighting because it is strictly forbidden at that level.

One of the tenets of the code has to do with fighting. When anyone mentions the code, any hockey fan will naturally think of the rules of combat between two fighters on the ice. We will get to the rules of engagement shortly, but first we must investigate the reasons why two players drop the gloves, as this is the beginning of the code as it relates to fighting.

The most common reason for fighting in hockey has always been retaliation and retribution. Since the beginning of hockey, some players have taken a few extra liberties with their sticks or given a cheap hit from behind. A fight might break out right then and there, or it might happen later in the season, but most fighting in hockey is based on revenge.

In the high-stakes realm of the National Hockey League, if one team's star player is taken out of the game or for a shift, revenge must be meted out (according to the code) or else the team will think they can get away with any misbehavior on the ice. This does not mean players go out and commit brazen acts of violence that completely contradict the rules of the code.

The perfect example of how retribution works is shown in the incident between Rene Bourque and Nicklas Backstrom. On January 4, 2012, Rene Bourque elbowed Washington Capitals superstar Nicklas Backstrom in the head, leaving Backstrom with a concussion and forcing him to sit out several games. Bourque earned a five-game suspension for the hit. Before his suspension was over, however, Bourque was traded to the Montreal Canadiens, and as luck would have it, his first game since his suspension was against the Washington Capitals.

Despite being in a new city, Bourque knew he would still have to answer for what he had done to the Capitals star, and on his first shift on the ice, Capitals Matt Hendricks exacted his vengeance on Bourque. Bourque had made the hit on Backstrom, and he had served his suspension, but the code still required him to answer for his actions. After that fight, the Capitals let the incident slide, knowing that their star player had been avenged.

Enforcers will also use intimidation or the fear of fighting to change the outcome of a game. The mere fact of having a player such as Tony Twist or Dave Schultz on the ice will force teams to think twice before doing anything to their opponent's players. The purpose of using enforcers is to provide space on the ice for the "better" players to maneuver and hopefully score goals. Players who don't want to get beaten up stay out of the way, making the enforcer a valuable member of the club. But enforcers aren't the only players to use intimidation.

A player like Gordie Howe used intimidation to give himself a little extra room out on the ice. One of the most glaring examples occurred in February 1959, when Howe fought the New York Rangers tough guy Lou Fontinato. In the fight, Howe suffered a broken finger and a cut above the eye, but Fontinato came out with the worst of it with a broken nose. After that fight, Howe won the respect (and fear) of opposing players, and word quickly spread through the league not to mess with "Mr. Hockey."

Another common reason for fights is simple— bad blood between players or between teams. This is an element of hockey that spectators enjoy watching. What would Montreal–Boston games be without a little extra pushing and shoving? What would Calgary–Edmonton games be like without the rivalry between the two clubs? And would the 2012 Pittsburgh–Philadelphia playoff series been as good as it was without Crosby proclaiming, "I don't like any guy on their team"?

Now that have we have established some of the reasons for fighting, the next part of the code relates to getting the job done. One of the first unspoken rules of engagement is to always fight within your weight class. This is a simple requirement to make sure that one guy is not at a distinct disadvantage in the battle. Imagine Georges Laraque (250 pounds, 6-foot-4) fighting Sidney Crosby (200 pounds, 5-foot-9), and you'll understand this rule.

Fighters tend to drop the gloves only against other enforcers, enacting the code within their small group, meaning that enforcers often end up fighting each other over something another player did on their team—a settling of accounts by proxy. However, this unwritten rule can get thrown out if a lightweight player takes a cheap shot on one of their opponents superstars; then an enforcer will automatically take the guy to task no matter what his size.

Another element of the code that every fighter must honor is when another player is injured before or during the fight—the injured player must be allowed to back out from the tussle. The role of the enforcer is one that invites injury, and many times during a season the opposing player could be nursing injuries ranging from cuts to broken fingers. These injuries might not be serious enough to keep him from playing, but they certainly force the player to back down from a fight. Every enforcer knows this and must respect when another guy cannot drop the gloves. Injuries occur to every enforcer in the league, so it is mutually beneficial to respect this particular part of the code.

This rule also applies to any fighter who gets injured during a fight—the injured fighter calls uncle, or the aggressor sees that the other fighter can no longer continue and stops the fight. This occurs over and over again in NHL fights: when a guy goes down because of a broken nose or happens to bust his hand during a fight, the two fighters will part ways or allow the linesmen to get between them. Discontinuing the fight is easier said than done, though, as the fighters are amped up on adrenaline. But, in the end, it is the responsibility of a fighter to stop in order to avoid any tragic circumstances.

"I fought Stu [Grimson] a couple of years ago," said former NHL enforcer Sandy McCarthy, "and he fell down in the beginning, and I let him get back up. It tells you something about a player's personality when he hits a guy when he's down. I've hit guys when they're trying to cover up or something, but I've never hit a guy when he's down."

The code is all about fighting fair. Besides not fighting a guy when he's injured, the code stipulates that certain rules of engagement must be followed to keep the fight clean and simple. Tactics such as head butting, biting, hair pulling and eye gouging are all frowned upon by the fighter class and will definitely put you on the list for retribution at the next possible moment. Beyond these limitations, it is pretty much open war once a fight starts.

Recently, enforcers have had to contend with players using a visor on their helmets. More players are wearing this piece of equipment to protect their eyes, but in a fight, if one player is wearing one and the other is not, the person wearing the visor has the advantage of having the top half of his face protected from punches. Most tough guys in the league do not use the visor, or an honorable player will remove his helmet before the tussle begins. As Don Cherry once stated, "I never, ever said 'Don't wear a visor.' What I said was if you're wearing a visor and you're going for safety, okay. But don't go around being a tough guy."

Apart from fighting, the code of hockey covers other areas of the game that if violated, can often lead to fighting. Any of the following acts are deemed a serious violation of the code and will get you a visit from the team tough guy. Spraying ice in a goalie's face, celebrating too much after a goal when your team is already winning, crossing the center ice line during warm-ups (this used to be a huge issue for some teams and led to several fights before a game even started), diving (which is considered cheap and cowardly and should remain in soccer), tricking a guy into fighting and shooting the puck after the whistle has gone.

One thing made clear from the code is that boundaries between the teams must be respected at all times, and any violation will be met with physical force. A great example of one team breaking the code of respecting boundaries came before game six of the Conference finals between the Montreal Canadiens and the Philadelphia Flyers on May 14, 1987. Throughout the series, Canadiens forwards Shayne Corson and Claude Lemieux liked to wait until all the players left the ice during the pre-game warm-up skate so they could put a few pucks into their opponent's net for good luck. The two players did not really think much of it, but the Flyers goaltender Chico Resch and tough guy Ed Hospodar took great exception to the invasion of their territory and stormed back out of their dressing room to chase down Corson and Lemieux to teach them a lesson.

Hospodar immediately jumped on Lemieux and started to rain blows on him as Lemieux tried to protect himself. It looked like the fight was coming to an end until Patrick Roy came out of the Canadiens dressing room followed by Habs tough guy Chris Nilan. The Flyers dressing room got wind of the scuffle, and within minutes, players from both dressing rooms ended up out on the ice. At first, the players were just talking it out, but then Canadiens tough guy John Kordic joined the melee, and the scene escalated.

The linesmen and the referees had to leave their dressing room to break up the brawl. After a bit of shoving, order was eventually restored and both teams were sent back to their dressing rooms to await the start of the game. The Canadiens ended up losing the game, and the series, to the Flyers. For the Flyers, the Canadiens had broken a code of respect, and they forced the Canadiens to pay for their actions.

This and the other examples in this chapter define the code, and for many players, although it is not something they can read about in any book, knowing the code is instinctive.

"The code is something that has always been around in hockey," said Tony Twist, in Ross Bernstein's book *The Code*. "As players, we have always had the opportunity to police ourselves in order to give ourselves and our teams the best opportunities to succeed. The code is not always about fighting either. It is about intimidation through respect."

~ Chapter 4 ~

The Greatest Fighters
in NHL History

---

*Fifty percent of the game is mental and the
other 50 percent is being mental. I've got that
part down, no problem.*

–Basil McRae, St. Louis Blues tough guy

Sprague Cleghorn: The First Fighter

A common belief of some people is that the
good old days of hockey was a time when
the game was played by gentleman and fighting
was a rare occurrence. Those people of course had
obviously never heard of Sprague Cleghorn, one of
the meanest and toughest terrors on the blue line
who fought his battles with his fists and his stick.

Cleghorn was born in the upscale Westmount
area of Montreal, but despite his aristocratic
upbringing, he was a tough-as-nails hockey
player. He began his professional hockey career
in 1910 as a member of the Renfrew Creamery

Kings of the National Hockey Association (NHA). After one season with Renfrew, Cleghorn was traded to the Montreal Wanderers where he spent six seasons and began to develop his reputation as a dirty player, especially in the many heated battles against rival clubs, the Montreal Canadiens and the Quebec Bulldogs.

After sitting out the inaugural NHL season in 1917–18 because of a leg injury, Cleghorn resumed his on-ice violence as a member of the Ottawa Senators. However, despite not playing clean, Cleghorn was also one of the best defensemen on the ice, helping the Senators to Stanley Cup victories in 1920 and in 1921. The major reason for his success as a defenseman was probably because many players were just afraid to get near him. His was a career defined by tales of his nasty temper. Another reason for his nastiness on the ice was related to his overprotective attitude toward his younger brother, Odie, a high-scoring winger who was Sprague's teammate with both the pre-NHL Montreal Wanderers and later with the Montreal Canadiens.

One of the first examples of Cleghorn's proclivity toward violence on the ice happened on December 12, 1912, when his Montreal Wanderers traveled to Toronto to play in an exhibition game against the Montreal Canadiens. At about the halfway point in the game, Montreal's superstar player Newsy Lalonde slammed Odie hard into the boards; Sprague saw red. After skating clear across the ice, Sprague drove his stick into Lalonde's forehead. Lalonde fell to the ice with blood pouring down his face, while the referees tried to separate the scrum of players that formed around him after the hit. Lalonde needed 12 stitches to close the gash on his head. Toronto police and prosecutors did not take kindly to Cleghorn's violent display for a simple exhibition game, so summoned him before the city court and fined him $50 in addition to the $50 levied against him by the National Hockey Association.

After winning the Stanley Cup with the Senators in 1921, Cleghorn was traded to the Montreal Canadiens, reuniting him with Odie. The Canadiens already had a lineup of future Hall of Famers, including Lalonde, Georges Vezina and Didier Pitre. But it was the pairing of Cleghorn and tough defenseman Billy Coutu that turned the Canadiens blue line into not only the most dominant defense in the league but also the scariest. Coutu holds the dubious distinction of being the only player to be banned from the NHL for life. During an incident while playing for the Boston Bruins, he punched a referee, tackled another and started a brawl in the 1927 Stanley Cup finals.

In Cleghorn's first season with the Canadiens, he established himself as the tough guy on

February 1, 1922, when he showed his teammates that he had not lost his edge. Playing the Senators that night, and still holding a grudge against the franchise for trading him, Cleghorn made it his mission to slash, punch and injure as many of his former teammates as possible. Cleghorn first unleashed his rage on Senators star defenseman Eddie Gerard with a vicious slash just above his eye, opening up a gash that required five stitches and knocking Gerard out of the game with a concussion. Cleghorn's next target was Ottawa sniper Frank Nighbor, who was caught off guard by a Cleghorn check that sent Nighbor sprawling to the ice, injuring his elbow and taking him out of the game. Cleghorn's final victim of the night was Senators star forward Cy Denneny who took a Cleghorn spear to the face that sent blood rushing out of his nose and all over the ice.

Naturally, the Senators were up in arms over the game and immediately appealed to NHL president Frank Calder to bar Cleghorn from the game for life, given the incident and his past transgressions. As was the custom in the NHL back then, the other general managers of the league brought Calder to a decision. Only a unanimous vote would see Cleghorn leave the league in disgrace, but both the Toronto St. Pats and the Hamilton Tigers voted against suspending Cleghorn.

Senators rookie Francis "King" Clancy had watched Cleghorn's vicious rampage that February night and later recalled the effect Cleghorn had on the game. "He was just a terrible man to have to play against, a terrific stick-handler, a master with the butt-end and tough. Holy Jesus, he was tough."

But Clancy had another run-in with the famous tough guy. In a game between the Senators and the Canadiens during the 1921–22 season, Cleghorn was rushing up the ice into the Senators zone when Clancy banged his stick on the ice, pretending to be a teammate asking for a pass. Without looking, Cleghorn sent the puck to Clancy, who proceeded to take his team down the opposite end of the ice, much to the delight of the Senators home crowd. When the period came to an end, the fans gave Clancy an extra bit of applause as he walked off the ice, and just as he was going into the dressing room, someone called his name. When Clancy turned around, all he saw was Cleghorn's fist coming at him.

In the 1923 playoffs, Cleghorn attacked another Ottawa Senators player so viciously that his own team suspended him, fearing what he might do next. Canadiens general manager Leo Dandurand described the incident as something "befitting an animal." However, it must be remembered that even among his violent outbursts, Cleghorn played solid hockey. He died in July 1956 as the result of a car accident in Montreal, and in 1958 he was posthumously inducted into the Hockey Hall of Fame. It's hard to reconcile Cleghorn's hockey skills with the man who was once arrested for beating his wife with a crutch in 1918, but Cleghorn resisted convention.

Cleghorn spent his final few years in the NHL with the Boston Bruins and helped guide and shape a young defenseman named Eddie Shore into becoming an equally tough and skilled player who soon made his own reputation in the league.

Eddie Shore: Old-school Tough

He was the epitome of the Big Bad Bruins. Hockey legend Eddie Shore may have possessed the greatest combination of skill and ferocious tyranny ever to put on skates in the NHL. He was a defenseman who could rush the puck up the ice like Bobby Orr, but unlike Orr, he had a mean streak in him that defied comprehension, fueled by his apprenticeship under Sprague Cleghorn and by his maniacally competitive nature.

Eddie Shore was born in 1902 on a farm in Fort Qu'Appelle, Saskatchewan. He toughened his body working for his father, hauling grain and slinging hay for hours on end. When he had time off, like most other young men, he enjoyed playing sports and excelled in baseball and soccer.

He only became interested in hockey around the age of 17 when his brother told him he could never be a great hockey player. Ever the competitor, Shore set out to prove his brother wrong, and by the time he was 22, he had joined the amateur Melville Millionaires for the 1923–24 season. After one year as an amateur, Shore turned pro, joining the Western Canada Hockey League (WCHL) with the Regina Capitals for the 1924–25 season. After the Capitals folded in the off-season, Shore joined up with the Edmonton Eskimos, also of the WCHL, for the 1925–26 season. Shore scored 12 goals for the Eskimos that year, a total unheard of during that era. He quickly became famous for his end-to-end rushes, skating by or through players like a freight train. His skill earned him the nickname "The Edmonton Express."

When the WHL disbanded in 1926, fortunately for Shore, the NHL was expanding into the United States. The Bruins were the first to join in the NHL in 1924, and the league added franchises in Detroit, New York and Chicago. In order to sell the game to the new audiences, general managers were looking for flamboyant, physical players who could bring crowds to their feet, and the Boston Bruins were lucky enough to get their hands on Shore.

Shore joined the Bruins lineup at the same time they acquired defensemen Billy Coutu and

Sprague Cleghorn from the Montreal Canadiens. During Boston's first practice, before the season started, Shore, who was trying to impress the coaching staff, wheeled and spun about the ice in front of the two veteran defensemen.

Coutu and Cleghorn did not take kindly to being shown up by a rookie, so for the entire practice, Coutu made it his mission to hurt Shore in every manner possible. Coutu body slammed, head-butted, elbowed and tackled Shore every chance he could, trying to beat the arrogant rookie into submission. But Shore kept getting back up and giving as good as he got. Coutu then tried the direct approach, ramming into Shore at full speed at center ice. Shore managed to hold his ground, sending Coutu through the air and crashing hard to the ice.

Coutu was forced off the ice for a week while Shore had his ear partially torn off in the collision. Shore left practice and walked around Boston looking for a doctor to reattach the dangling ear. When he found a physician, Shore refused the anesthetic and watched in a mirror as the doctor reattached his ear, making sure the doctor did his best not to leave a scar.

"I was just a farm boy who didn't want his looks messed up," Shore joked later. "I made him change the last stitch; he would have left a scar!"

With a display of toughness like that, Shore earned the respect of his teammates and more importantly, a spot on the Bruins. In his rookie season, he again scored 12 goals and also racked up 130 minutes in penalties, second most in the league. The following year, in 1927–28, Shore set a new NHL record with 165 penalty minutes, all while scoring 11 goals; it was the second of five-straight seasons in which he topped the 10-goal plateau.

Shore's toughness was not just in his fists but in his physique. He routinely played upwards of 50 to 55 minutes during a 60-minute game. This kind of heart and passion for his team quickly found Shore a loyal following in Boston, and his star power grew even more when he led the Bruins to an undefeated playoff run to give the franchise its first Stanley Cup victory in 1928–29.

Despite his all-star status and shiny new Stanley Cup ring, Shore still had fire in his game. In fact, over the next few years, his rage on the ice only grew stronger.

The season after his Stanley Cup win, Shore established a far more notorious league mark that is almost sure never to be broken. On November 23, 1929, Shore was assessed five fighting majors in a single game against the Montreal Maroons. The carnage began with a tussle against the Maroons Buck Boucher, and as Shore skated off to the penalty box after the fight, he took it upon himself to butt-end Montreal's Dave Trottier in the face. After that fight, it seemed the goal of entire Maroons lineup was to get back at Shore, and he was more than happy to oblige. Late in the third period, the referees had to stop the game because every time Shore was on the ice, a fight broke out. By the end of the game, Shore, Boucher and the Maroons Albert "Babe" Siebert were all hospitalized. Shore left the hospital with a broken nose, four missing teeth, two black eyes, a concussion and numerous cuts and scrapes.

Games like that were a common occurrence for Shore and the Bruins because teams figured if you could beat Shore, you could beat the Bruins.

Shore's most infamous moment came during the 1933–34 season in a game against the Toronto Maple Leafs on December 12, 1933. The game was like any other—the Leafs targeting Shore every chance they could. During the second period, Shore took off on one of his trademark end-to-end rushes and just as he entered the Toronto zone, he was blindsided by Leafs defenseman King Clancy. Enraged, Shore picked himself up and scanned the ice for the most likely culprit. Unfortunately, the closest Leaf player happened to be the innocent Ace Bailey. Shore skated straight toward the unsuspecting Bailey and leveled him with a vicious hit from behind that sent him sprawling to the ice.

Toronto assistant general manager Frank Selke was there that night and later recounted the sequence of events.

Shore arose and slowly started back to his end of the playing arena. He was behind Red Horner and Bailey. Whether he mistook Bailey for Clancy, or whether he was annoyed by his own futility and everything in general, we will never know. But we all saw Shore put his head down and rush at top speed. He struck Bailey across the kidneys with his right shoulder and with such a force that it upended Bailey in a backward somersault, while the powerful Shore kept right on going.

Leafs defenseman Red Horner saw Bailey laying on the ice, and in a rage, he skated over to Shore and clocked him with a hard right to the jaw, knocking him out cold. Bailey, who was at the other end, was in serious trouble. He was taken to the dressing room convulsing, so the trainers packed his head in ice to reduce the swelling and rushed him to the hospital. Doctors immediately knew that Bailey had suffered a fractured skull. Over the next six days, Bailey's life hung in the balance as doctors performed two risky brain surgeries to save his life. Meanwhile, Shore was brought into Boston police headquarters to face questioning about the incident. It was made clear to him that if Bailey died, he would be charged with manslaughter. The hockey world waited with baited breath for any news of Bailey's condition. Luckily for Bailey, and for Shore, Bailey stepped out of danger and began the long road to recovery. But Bailey never played hockey again .

Shore received a 16-game suspension, but the trauma of that day stayed with Shore as he was racked by feelings of guilt. However, two months later at an all-star fundraiser on February 14, 1934, held in Bailey's honor, the two players shook hands in public, making it clear there were no hard feelings.

Shore played in the NHL for another six years, winning a second Stanley Cup in 1939 before hanging up his skates in 1940.

At the end of Shore's rough but illustrious career, he had received 978 stitches and his nose was broken 14 times and his jaw five times. He also spent 1037 minutes in the penalty box over his 14 NHL seasons, an impressive figure today, but an astronomical one in the 1930s. More importantly, although many people hated Shore for his vicious streak, fans loved him for it, and no matter how you felt about him, you couldn't deny that he was a talented player, something lacking in many modern tough guys.

Ted Lindsay: "Terrible" Ted

Although Ted Lindsay did not have the natural talent of his Detroit Red Wings linemate Gordie Howe, he more than made up for the deficit with his sheer grit and nastiness, making him one of the hardest players to knock off the puck. Let's just say he earned his nickname of "Scarface" the hard way.

Considerably smaller than his linemate Gordie Howe, Lindsay was no less tenacious and scrappy. From 1949 to about 1956, the two players combined their skills to terrorize their opponents and keep Detroit at the top during that time. The two star wingers first played with Sid Abel at center, and later with Alex Delvecchio, to form what was dubbed the "Production Line," a tribute to Detroit's automotive industry. The nickname related to their line's scoring prowess, but it also referred to both Lindsay and Howe regularly running roughshod over their opponents. Lindsay especially excelled at the more physical side of the game, a rare combination of player who could both score and fight. Only a handful of tough guys in the league could put together a few seasons where their scoring ability matched their physical dominance. Lindsay spent seven straight seasons in the top 10 scoring leaders and equaled that top ten placement among the most penalized.

Lindsay's tough-guy persona could be traced back to his youth in Renfrew, Ontario, as the youngest of nine children. He learned hockey playing against his five older brothers who never took it easy on him just because he was the baby of the family. When World War II broke out and his older brothers left to serve their country, 15-year-old Lindsay had no one to practice with, but by then he had toughened up and was making waves in the amateur hockey clubs near his home. While he was playing for the junior St. Michael's College hockey team, a Red Wings scout noticed his particular brand of hockey and signed him to a contract.

Lindsay paid his dues in the Red Wings farm team before joining the club for the 1944–45 season as a fresh-faced 19-year-old rookie. Right from the start, it was clear that Lindsay was not interested in making friends but only in winning hockey games. During a game against the Toronto Maple Leafs, Lindsay viciously went after defenseman Gus Mortson the entire game, slashing, checking and butt-ending whenever he could, despite the fact that they were childhood friends, former junior teammates and business partners at the time.

"I don't know anybody when a hockey game starts," Lindsay once famously said of his playing style.

Lindsay fought when he had to, but he was most well known for frequently using his stick, elbows, knees and fists to get any advantage he could. His "win-at-all-costs" attitude earned him the moniker, "Terrible Ted," and the prodigious use of his elbows and his stick led the NHL to instate penalties for kneeing and elbowing.

Although Lindsay was a key element in the Detroit Red Wings' success and one of the major reasons they won four Stanley Cups, his combative nature off the ice broke up the Production Line. In the mid-1950s, Lindsay was at the forefront of a movement to get NHL players to organize into a union to protect their interests. However, at the time, the team owners operated like a dictatorship and were quick to strike down Lindsay's efforts to organize. As punishment, in the summer of 1957, the Detroit Red Wings traded Lindsay to the Chicago Blackhawks, the team that had finished last overall in the standings the previous season.

Lindsay managed to put in three seasons with the Blackhawks, but he was not happy in his new uniform, which might have caused the spike in his seasonal penalty minutes. He achieved a career-high and a league-high 184 penalty minutes in the 1958–59 season.

After three seasons with the Hawks, Lindsay decided to retire from the game he loved. He was

a Red Wing at heart and could not continue playing if he didn't believe in his team. Lindsay was
content in his decision and focused on his business interests in Detroit, while watching games
at home. But the desire to compete never left
him, and when he was asked to come out of
retirement for the 1964–65 season to join the
Red Wings, he jumped at the chance to put on
the red jersey again. And just like old times, during his first game back against the Toronto Maple
Leafs, Ted Lindsay got up to his old tricks.

"I couldn't let the fans down. I was pretty
pumped up when the game started. It felt like old
times again. The fans cheering us on, the sights
and smells of the arena—and I even got into
a fight with Tim Horton and drew a 10-minute
misconduct."

Lindsay scored 14 goals and 14 assists in 69
games that season. But most importantly, he
drew 173 penalty minutes, the second-highest
total of his career, proving that even at 40 years
old and after four years out the of the league, no
one could take the fight out of Terrible Ted.

Maurice Richard: Eyes of Fire

Maurice "The Rocket" Richard is known for
his goal scoring and rightfully so; he was the first
player to score 50 goals in 50 games and held several other scoring records for decades. He was the

face of the Montreal Canadiens through their glory days in the 1950s and was lauded as a symbol of the French-speaking population in Quebec. Although he deserves to be remembered for all his incredible exploits, Maurice Richard also had a darker side.

Scoring 50 goals in 50 games is an incredible accomplishment that few in the NHL have achieved since, but records like that garner you added attention from the opposition every time you step out on the ice. Players tried everything to slow Richard down on his famous offensive rushes, but he was no pushover and could give an elbow and a slash and could fight with the toughest in the league.

Maurice Richard was born the eldest of eight children to working-class parents on August 4, 1921. He grew up in north Montreal during the Depression, spending most of his time involved in sports. Richard was a good baseball player and loved boxing, but it was hockey that stirred his passions. He played hockey whenever he could, moving up the ranks of the local leagues before finally getting his big break with the Canadiens in 1942.

Initially, the Canadiens did not want to take a chance on the young Richard because he had broken his leg in junior hockey and all the scouts had tagged him as a fragile player. At Richard's first practice with the Canadiens, general manager and head coach Dick Irvin knew that Richard had fire in his eyes and a determination that could one day make him a leader on the team. But the Habs were still unsure whether Richard could hold up against the rigors of the larger and meaner NHL players, so at practice they decided to test Richard's metal.

The task was handed to veteran Murph Chamberlain, a forward with a knack for the more physical side of the game. Over and over again during practice, Chamberlain took shot after shot on Richard, running him hard into the boards and slashing at him when he could. After Chamberlain rammed him hard into the boards, Richard lost his temper and went straight for Chamberlain with his fists clenched. Richard sent the big forward reeling with a hard right to the jaw. It took three teammates to remove Richard from his hefty inquisitor. Canadiens general manager Tommy Gorman and Irvin knew in that moment that they had found a player to work with and signed him to a contract.

Life in the NHL only got tougher for Richard. After putting together a string of record-breaking seasons, including scoring 50 goals in 50 games and leading the Canadiens to the Stanley Cup, Richard became enemy number one to all opposing teams. But try as they might, no one could stop Richard.

During a game on February 3, 1945, against the Detroit Red Wings, big defenseman Earl Siebert was tasked with slowing Richard down any way he could. On one particular play, Richard sped past everyone except Siebert on a rush into the zone. Siebert tried to cut off Richard's path into the offensive zone, but the speedy forward was moving too quickly, so Siebert did the only thing he could think of; he wrapped his arms around Richard shoulders. It didn't work. Richard simply dug his skates in harder and continued on his path to the net. Siebert was literally riding Richard, but Richard could not be stopped.

Later, when recalling the incident, Richard said, "I felt his skates lifting off the ice and flying up in the air. I think he weighed about 210 pounds. I felt as if I might cave in. The goaltender moved straight out for me, and somehow I managed to jab the puck between his legs while Siebert kept riding my back."

Richard did not throw down the gloves often, but when he did, he could stand up against the toughest fighters. During a game against the New York Rangers early in Richard's career, management had brought in Bob Dill to shadow the Canadiens star forward and to goad him into fighting to take him out of the match. Dill had a reputation as a hard as nails fighter and a goon. Dill did what he could to get at Richard, but The Rocket kept his cool through the slashing and verbal assaults. When the two started a scuffle behind the net, Richard finally had had enough and dropped his gloves to take care of Dill.

Coach Irvin was screaming at Richard from the bench to get him out of the fight, but The Rocket was determined to settle the score his way. Dill tossed off his gloves and skated toward Richard. Without hesitation, Richard swung a hard right and put Dill on his knees. As the referee was ushering Richard toward the penalty box, Dill skated by Richard and slapped him in the face, sending The Rocket into a fury. When Dill was put into the penalty box, Richard jumped over to his side and began pummeling the Ranger while Dill sat inside the penalty box.

"All I could see from the other side were the Rocket's arms swinging madly," recalled former Canadiens trainer Ernie Cook. "When it finally stopped, I ran around to the penalty box from our bench figuring Maurice might want some attention. Just as I got there, Harry Westerby, the old Rangers trainer, was coming out. 'How is my man?' I asked Harry."

"He hasn't a scratch! But look at my man," roared Westerby, pointing to Dill, who was walking to the dressing room with two ice packs on his face, covering a mass of welts and bruises from Richard's flying fists.

Richard answered the call to drop the gloves more than once in his career, but the fight he was most famous for happened on March 13, 1955, in a game against the Boston Bruins. The Canadiens had beaten the Bruins two nights before in a physical game where the Bruins had paid particular attention to Richard, hacking and slashing at him whenever they could. Richard was used to this sort of treatment, but after nearly a full season of abuse with referees averting their eyes to the obvious penalties, Richard was on the edge.

During this game, one player in particular was getting on Richard's last nerve—defenseman Hal Laycoe. Several times in the first period, Laycoe hacked and slashed at Richard as The Rocket tried to break in on goal. Richard stared at his adversary with deep animosity in his cold eyes. The crowd sensed that something was going happen between the two men. And it did. The Rocket came blazing through the neutral zone and found only one player between him and the net—Hal Laycoe. As Richard tried to break out into the open, Laycoe grabbed onto Richard and pushed him into the corner. Laycoe then cross-checked Richard in the back of the head. The referee had already raised his arm to signal a penalty, but when Richard felt the blood trickling down his neck, he flew into a rage.

Clearly moved by nothing but fury, Richard swung his stick at Laycoe, hitting him first in the shoulder then deflecting into his face. Laycoe immediately dropped his stick and gloves, ready to settle the score. Richard was about to swing his stick again at Laycoe, but linesman Cliff Thompson intervened and took the weapon away. Richard found another stick in the chaos that was forming around him as other players joined in the fray. Again Richard wanted to hack at Laycoe with the stick, but this time linesman Thompson used a more forceful means to subdue Richard by pinning his arms behind his back.

While Richard was being held back, Laycoe seized the opportunity to sucker punch the defenseless player in the jaw. Richard was livid, and he warned the linesman to let him go, but when he broke loose, Thompson quickly grabbed him again, preventing him from reaching Laycoe. Another Montreal player who saw Richard being unfairly held back, bumped into the linesman, giving Richard the chance to free himself. Instead of going after Laycoe, Richard turned and punched linesman Thompson in the face twice.

"He wouldn't listen. That's why I hit him," said Richard about the fight.

When order was eventually restored, Richard was given a match penalty for his numerous violations, while Laycoe was handed a five-minute major for injuring Richard and a 10-minute misconduct for not going to the penalty box when asked. Things were about to get much worse for Richard, when a few days later he was suspended for the remainder of the season and the playoffs. The suspension, deemed unfair by Canadiens fans, touched off a riot on March 17, 1955, that caused about $1 million in property damages in the city of Montreal, in what would come to be known as the "Richard Riots." Richard ended the 1954–55 season with a career-high 125 penalty minutes.

Richard played hockey until the end of the 1959–60 season, finishing his career on a high note with a fifth consecutive Stanley Cup. He had lost some of the fire in his eyes by the end of his career, but The Rocket's fans will never forget the intensity he brought to each game he played.

John Ferguson: The First Enforcer

Although all kinds of fighters have played in the NHL, the concept of the enforcer is a relatively new one to hockey. Before the advent of the designated tough guy, stars such as Maurice Richard, Gordie Howe and Bobby Hull were forced to fight their own battles. They were good fighters, but it was better to have Howe or Richard on the ice scoring goals than risking their bodies by dropping the gloves. Teams often hired players simply to fight, but the idea of designating one guy to guard the star players did not really surface until the early 1960s when Montreal Canadiens general manager Frank Selke brought in a player to shield his star forward Jean Beliveau.

That man was John Ferguson, a mean-tempered hockey player from the American Hockey League who prided himself on being the nastiest player out on the ice. He developed that tough exterior at nine years old when he lost his father and grew up in the poorest neighborhood in Vancouver, the infamous East Hastings. As an only child, Ferguson had to become the man of his household at a young age, helping his overworked mother with chores and taking care of himself.

Yet despite his heavy responsibilities, John always made time for sports. At the age of 12, he was already laying the groundwork for his future NHL status when he joined a local boxing club for boys. He also became an elite player in lacrosse, a sport not known for the faint of heart or the physically weak. At 6 feet and around 200 pounds, he was not an easy opponent. When he discovered hockey at age 14, he knew he had found his passion. Although a late arrival to the sport, John proved to be rather adept at the game for such a large young man. When he wasn't on the ice practicing, he was working as a stick boy for the Vancouver Canucks of the Western Hockey League (WHL).

One night during the 1954–55 WHL season, as Ferguson sat behind the bench to watch his Canucks take on the Edmonton Flyers, he witnessed an incident that marked his future career in hockey.

The Edmonton Flyers boasted one of the toughest players in the league, a defenseman named Larry Zeidel. Vancouver's best player that season was Phil Maloney, who at one point ended up in the penalty box alongside Zeidel. In those days, opposing players often sat inside the same penalty box separated only by a league official. After Maloney and Zeidel exchanged a few words, Ferguson watched as Zeidel suddenly sucker punched Maloney in the jaw, and the worst part was that none of the Canucks came to the aid of their teammate.

"That always stayed in the back of my mind," Ferguson said. "I told myself that nobody would ever have to worry about me not protecting my teammates."

Ferguson carried that moment with him throughout his junior hockey career, until one fateful day when as a member of the Cleveland Barons of the American Hockey League (AHL), he found Larry Zeidel playing for the AHL's Hershey Bears. In the first game they played against each other, Ferguson dropped his gloves and pounded on Zeidel on the ice and later a second time in the penalty box, perhaps exorcising his demons from years past.

Ferguson's instinct to protect got him signed with the Montreal Canadiens for the start of the 1963–64 season. One year earlier, Jean Beliveau had had one of his worst years statistically. He was hounded by the league's less talented players and was unable to perform his offensive magic. Beliveau could handle himself out on the ice, but he was not about to drop his gloves and go at it with the NHL's goons.

Placed on a line with Beliveau and Bernard Geoffrion for the opening game of the 1963–64 season against the Boston Bruins, Ferguson took all of 12 seconds from the opening faceoff to engage in a punch-up with the Bruins "Terrible" Ted Green. The rookie had arrived in the league and made it known that the Canadiens' stars were off-limits. Ferguson's impact was immediate. Jean Beliveau went from scoring just 18 goals in the previous season to 28, and he was now free from having to defend himself. Beliveau went from 78 penalty minutes in the previous season to just 43 after the arrival of Ferguson.

The difference between Ferguson and most of the enforcers in the league today is that he also had a scoring touch. Hands that normally pound faces are not known for their ability to deftly handle the puck, but Ferguson signaled in his first game with the Canadiens that he could play—he potted two goals and got an assist. Placed on the line with Beliveau and Geoffrion certainly helped his game, but Ferguson held his own. In fact, he was near the top of the league in scoring when his proclivity for fighting knocked him out of the game for some time in the most gruesome of ways.

In the latter half of his rookie season, the Canadiens were playing the Boston Bruins again, and this time Ferguson found himself in a scrap with Ed Westfall. Ferguson was well known in the league for continuing to throw punches even when his victims were down or covered by the linesmen. That mean streak got him into trouble this time.

"I knocked him down and went to punch him again, but he put his skate up and I punched right through his skate," recalled Ferguson. "My thumb was hanging on by its skin."

Ferguson was rushed to the hospital and doctors managed to sew his thumb back on. He only missed 18 games before returning to the lineup.

The next season continued as before, with Ferguson scoring goals and punching faces, but it was a fight in game five of the 1965 Stanley Cup finals against the Chicago Blackhawks that many would remember. After going into the Blackhawks zone, Ferguson got mixed up in the corner with tough guy Eric Nesterenko. The play continued as usual until Nesterenko slashed his stick over Ferguson's head. Ferguson responded in kind, dropping his gloves and pounding Nesterenko in the face, hitting him twice in the face before Nesterenko fell to the ice, unconscious.

Ferguson was not known for giving up pursuit of his challengers and continued to pound Nesterenko while he was down, opening up a cut on his forehead that covered the ice in blood. Ferguson was sent to the box, and Nesterenko eventually woke up but did not play the rest of the game. The Canadiens ended up winning the Stanley Cup series in the seventh game.

"John Ferguson had no conscience," said former coach and *Hockey Night in Canada* broadcaster Harry Neale. "Even some of the toughest players have had a conscience. They knew when they had gone too far, and they were sorry they did. Not John Ferguson. A lot of guys who fight like the fighting, but they don't want to hurt anyone. Ferguson would hurt you."

Ferguson also carried his nasty temperament with him off the ice, and if you were not his teammate, he did not want to know you. While other players in the league remained friendly with their opposing players, taking part in various golf tournaments and attending charity events, Ferguson always politely declined if anyone other than his teammates were present. Once, while eating dinner at a restaurant, Ferguson got up and walked out in the middle of his meal when he saw Toronto Maple Leafs tough guy Eddie Shack walk in.

Ferguson was so good at his job as a fighter that he was offered the chance to fight an exhibition bout with Canadian heavyweight champion George Chuvalo, who twice went toe to toe with the greatest boxer of all time, Muhammad Ali, without being knocked out. But when Canadiens general manager Sam Pollock got wind of the fight, he put a stop to it, fearing what might happen to his player. Ferguson was tough, but Chuvalo was a pro.

Following eight years, all spent with the Canadiens, five Stanley Cups and eight consecutive years of over 100 penalty minutes, Ferguson retired at the end of the 1970–71 season. After so many fights and so many bloodied faces, Ferguson's conscience finally caught up with him. "That's really the thing that made me retire," he explained. "I thought I was going to hurt someone badly in a fight."

But Ferguson never truly left hockey behind, becoming general manager of the New York Rangers and then the Winnipeg Jets, who were part of the World Hockey Association and eventually the NHL. Ferguson lost only one fight in his life; cancer took him from the world in 2007 at the age of 68.

Dave "Tiger" Williams: The Showman

You consent to assault when you lace up your skates. It's what hockey is all about.

–Tiger Williams

Not many enforcers in the NHL can boast of their consistency and longevity in the league like Dave "Tiger" Williams can. From 1974 to 1988, Williams played in 962 games, averaging about 20 goals and 300 minutes in penalties per season.

Williams' love for the more physical aspect of the game was identified at an early age. His first minor league hockey coach in his hometown of Weyburn, Saskatchewan, gave Williams the nickname "Tiger" because of the fiery temperament and ferocity he displayed on the ice. At the time, Williams was only five years old.

Tiger started playing junior hockey for the Swift Current Broncos of the Western Hockey

League (WHL) in the 1971–72 season. He did not score many goals, but his physical presence on the ice got him the most attention; he tallied 278 penalty minutes. The following season, however, Williams' scoring touch was ignited when he was put alongside a young Bryan Trottier. Over the next two seasons with the Broncos, Williams scored 96 goals and had 114 assists for 210 points in 134 games, all the while continuing his role as an enforcer.

Numbers like that naturally caught the attention of many of the National Hockey League's general managers who were hoping they had found themselves another John Ferguson, making Williams one of the top prospects at the 1974 Entry Draft. However, a scouting report on his awkward skating style led teams to pass him up, until the Toronto Maple Leafs selected him 31st overall.

After half a season spent with the Leafs' farm team, Williams got called up to The Bigs. Placed on the Leafs' top line with Darryl Sittler and Ron Ellis, Williams was given the tools to succeed and did not let his teammates down, scoring 10 goals and 19 assists in 42 games and tallying 187 penalty minutes.

Over the next four seasons with the Leafs, Williams continued to take on the NHL's toughest challengers, leading the league in fighting majors in three of those years and all the while managing 40 or more points. Not a bad record considering he was in the sin bin for an average of 320 penalty minutes per year.

For the most part, Williams was a fair and clean fighter who respected the unwritten code. But hockey can sometimes get the better of a player's rational side, and an incident on October 20, 1976, almost landed him in jail. That night, the Leafs were playing the Pittsburgh Penguins in Toronto, and during a fracas with the Pens Dennis Owchar, Williams viciously slashed him in the head. The resulting gash left a horrific scene of blood on the ice, and Owchar required 46 stitches to close the wound in his head.

The Department of Justice in Ontario got wind of the incident, judged the hit to be outside the normal boundaries of NHL violence and filed assault charges against Williams for which he was eventually acquitted.

Another one of Williams' not-so-proud moments came in the 1976 playoffs in a game against the Philadelphia Flyers. In the third period of game six, an all-out brawl started after Williams and Bobby Clarke exchanged a few high sticks. The Flyers enforcer, the notable Dave "The Hammer" Schultz, quickly came to the aid of his number one player and paired up with Williams. They spent most of their battle in close quarters swapping a few weak punches before the linesmen separated them. Amazingly, it was the only fight ever between the two heavyweights considering that they both played most of their careers at the same time and were such noted brawlers.

After the game, Flyers GM Keith Allen brought NHL president Clarence Campbell down to the Flyers locker room to show him the bite mark on Schultz's cheek given by Williams. Williams did not receive any supplemental discipline from the league for the incident.

During the 1979–80 season with the Leafs, Williams was having a career year. In 55 games, he scored 22 goals and had 18 assists. Earlier in the season, he went up against one of the toughest players in the league—Dave Semenko of the Edmonton Oilers, Wayne Gretzky's noted protector. After meeting behind the Leafs net, Williams and Semenko sized each other up and dropped their gloves for a fight not soon forgotten. People knew Tiger Williams was tough, but Semenko looked more the part with his huge hulking frame, thick neck and steel-like jaw. Once each threw a few punches, Williams caught Semenko in the jaw with a devastating blow that knocked Semenko to one knee. Down but not out, Semenko quickly rose to his feet, swinging away, but Williams had the advantage and hit him with a massive uppercut that sent Semenko to the ice for good with a bloodied lip and nose. After downing Semenko, Williams was without question the number one pugilist in the league.

Shortly afterward, however, despite Williams' surging stats, the Leafs traded Williams to the Vancouver Canucks along with Jerry Butler in return for Rick Vaive and Bill Derlago.

Williams disapproved of the swift trade, but he was determined to make new fans out west. In his first game with the Canucks against the Flyers, Williams got into three fights and caused a bench-clearing brawl that resulted in a total of 344 penalty minutes being handed out. He had the fans already, but his defining moment as a Canuck and as a player came later in the 1979–80 season in his first game back in Toronto against his former club.

As luck would have it, late in the game with the score tied, Williams rushed in on goal on a break, took a pass and popped in the game-winning goal. But it was his celebration afterward that became his trademark. After scoring, Williams turned back to the open ice, put his stick between his legs and rode it like a horse down the ice, pointing to the Leafs bench and to the fans, as if to say, "That's what you get for trading me!" Although he celebrated a goal like that only once in his career, it became one of the most memorable scoring celebrations and a signature move of

Tiger Williams that was shown decades later on the top ten lists of ESPN and TSN.

With Williams providing the Canucks with an added boost of energy, they just made the play-offs and came up against the mighty Buffalo Sabres in the first round. The Sabres had finished the season with 110 points as compared with the Canucks' 70, and they were coached by the legendary Scotty Bowman.

A series win was a long shot for the Canucks, but Williams pushed hard every shift to pester the Sabres' top players. Things got a little out of hand in the third game of the best-of-five series during a scuffle in front of the Sabres bench when Williams, who naturally was at the center of the melee, hit coach Bowman in the head with his stick.

Williams always denied it, but Bowman told a different story, saying, "It was a real two-hander." No one on the ice witnessed the assault, but an NHL executive watching the game from his luxury seat saw the infraction, and after the game, suspended Williams. The Canucks ended up losing the next game and the series.

The 1980–81 season was the best of Williams' career. He led the Canucks with a career-high 35 goals and led the league in penalty minutes with 343 in 77 games. He was named to the All-Star game, and true to form, he ended up knocking superstar Mike Bossy to the ice with a solid check.

Williams continued his on-ice antics with the Canucks until the 1983–84 season before being traded to the Detroit Red Wings. After half a season with the Wings, Williams was sent down to the minors. The Los Angeles Kings then picked him up for the start of the 1984–85 season. Williams had two good seasons with the Kings, scoring 16 goals in the first and 20 goals in the second before age finally began to catch up with him.

After leaving Los Angeles, Williams played 26 games for the Hartford Whalers in the 1987–88 season before hanging up his skates and putting his fists away for good. In 962 games played, he scored 241 goals and 272 assists and posted a NHL record 3966 penalty minutes.

Dave Schultz: The Broad Street Bully

I'd rather fight than score.

–Dave "The Hammer" Schultz

The Philadelphia Flyers of the 1970s, were mean, tough and unpleasant to play against, earning them the nickname "The Broad Street Bullies." While other teams such as the Montreal Canadiens and the Buffalo Sabres relied on skilled offensive players Guy Lafleur, Steve Shutt,

Rene Robert and Gilles Perreault to win games, the Flyers relied on their sheer ability to offend.

With notable tough guys like Andre "Moose" Dupont, Bob "Hound Dog" Kelly and Don "Big Bird" Saleski, the Flyers pounded their opponents into submission and turned that into two Stanley Cups. But no one epitomized the true spirit of the Broad Street Bullies era more than Dave Schultz, a cantankerous tough guy who once appeared on the cover of *Philadelphia* magazine wearing a soldier's helmet and holding a daisy, with the caption "This is Dave Schultz. He Loves You Not."

As tough as he was on the ice, Schultz did not have the upbringing that many people equate with that of an enforcer, such as coming from a broken home, failing in school, bullying smaller kids or often being in trouble with the police. Growing up in rural Saskatchewan, Schultz's early life was pretty tame. In school, he was a quiet kid who kept to himself, and when he started playing hockey, he was known more for his goal-scoring prowess than for fighting. Many of the fighters or tough guys in the NHL don't usually start out that way as youngsters. A common story for these kinds of players is that because of their size, they could out-muscle their opponents, which often led them to become good scorers. Schultz had the same background.

After graduating from a backyard rink hockey with his brothers, Schultz moved up through the rankings, eventually joining the junior hockey Swift Current Broncos, where in two seasons he scored 51 goals and had 51 assists in 92 games. Although he earned 200 penalty minutes during that period, he got into only two fights; most of his penalty minutes were the result of his aggressive approach to the game.

Schultz's aggressive style and deft scoring touch caught the attention of the Philadelphia Flyers, who selected Schultz in the fifth round of the 1969 Entry Draft. It was also the year that the Flyers selected Bobby Clarke and Don "Big Bird" Saleski. The Flyers were building a tough team for the future.

Schultz made it through the Flyers' training camp but still needed some conditioning to make it to the NHL. He played with the Salem Valley Rebels of the rough-and-tumble Eastern Hockey League, the same league that served as the inspiration for the cult hockey classic film *Slap Shot*. Schultz quickly learned that he could affect the flow and outcome of a game not only with his stick but with his fists. In his first game with Salem, he got into two fights, and from then on, he evolved into a different type of hockey player.

Schultz finished the 1969–70 season with 32 goals, 37 assists and 356 penalty minutes in

67 games. "We had some big guys on our team, but no one who seemed to want to fight," Schultz recounted. "So I quickly became that guy. The fans started cheering for and wanting it; I kind of enjoyed that. I didn't enjoy the fighting, but I enjoyed the rewards. So I just concentrated on that, but I still wanted to play hockey."

Schultz spent one year in the Eastern Hockey League, then the Flyers moved him up to their top minor league farm team, the Quebec Aces of the American Hockey League (AHL). Schultz led the AHL with 382 penalty minutes, double the amount of the next-highest player. After another year in the minors, Schultz finally got his chance in the NHL.

A few games into Schultz's first NHL season, the Flyers played host to the Chicago Blackhawks and their tough defenseman, Keith Magnuson. Schultz took the first opportunity he had at goading Magnuson into a fight by nailing him a hard check behind the net in the first period. Schultz knew that Magnuson had to answer the call to fight sometime in the game. Magnuson did not wait long. Right after the ensuing faceoff, Magnuson headed straight at Schultz, and the two heavyweights dropped their gloves. Anyone who watches hockey knows that Flyers fans love fights, and in just one game, Schultz made a lot of his own fans.

Game by game, Flyers head coach Fred Shero, Schultz and the rest of the team built their persona, and Schultz's was established early in his rookie season by Philadelphia Bulletin reporter Jack Chevalier. After a game where Schultz had a particularly dominant fight, Chevalier gushed like a fan over Schultz, exclaiming, "Boy, did you ever hammer that guy." From that moment on, Dave Schultz would forever be known as "The Hammer."

Schultz finished the 1972–73 season with 9 goals, 12 assists and 259 minutes in penalties. Coincidentally, it was also the first year the Flyers made the playoffs since joining the league in 1967. They also won their first series, beating the Minnesota North Stars in six games before losing to the Montreal Canadiens in the second round.

Schultz had the best season of his career in 1973–74, with 20 goals, 16 assists and 348 penalty minutes. In the playoffs that year, the Flyers swept the Atlanta Flames in the first round, then beat the New York Rangers in seven games in the second and finally managed to beat the Boston Bruins—a team that had an equally bad reputation for on-ice violence as the Flyers—in the Stanley Cup finals for the franchise's first championship.

During the Flyers' 17 games on their way to the Cup, Schultz racked up 139 minutes in penalties—an average of eight minutes per game—along with two goals and four assists.

Despite the Flyers' successes on the ice, other teams in the league did not appreciate their physical intimidation tactics, and the Broad Street Bullies gained many critics in the hockey world. "The newspapers would be telling people to hide the women and children because the animals were coming," Schultz said. "'The Broad Street Bullies' themselves, with our team having a nickname, we fed off that, I suppose. But the key was that we had a great team."

The Flyers continued to pound their opponents into submission for the 1974–75 season and carried that momentum into the playoffs for another Stanley Cup victory. It was also the year Schultz made NHL history. Other teams had caught on to the Flyers' aggressive tactics, and in order to challenge the team, the tough guys made a point of taking the Flyers' toughest player to task. As a result, Schultz racked up a ridiculous total of 472 penalty minutes in 76 games, a record that will likely never be broken. Broken down, that means 61 minor penalties, 26 fighting majors and 22 misconducts. In a single game that year, Schultz was assessed a total of 58 minutes worth of penalties with two minors, two fighting majors, one 10-minute misconduct and a 34-minute game misconduct.

One of the reasons Schultz was such a good fighter was that he went into each game prepared. After injuring his wrist in a fight, he put boxing wraps on his hands to protect them from damage in future games. However, once the injury healed, Schultz continued to wrap his hands, to prevent further injury. Soon, tough guys around the league were wrapping their hands before games, but the NHL quickly put a stop to this practice by installing what became known as the "Schultz Rule"—boxing wraps were banned from the league for fear that it gave the fighters an advantage and could cause more serious injuries than a bare fist.

As dominant as Schultz was on the ice with his fists, behind the tough guy exterior was a complex man who did not always have the desire to step into the ring. At first, he loved to go into a town and hear the fans screaming for him to fight, but in time, he was reluctant to fight.

"There were times when I didn't want to look at the schedule to know we were into, say, Boston in two weeks. I didn't want to know that, I didn't want to have to think about it," Schultz said. "If a team didn't really have a guy that was going to stand up to me, it just made it so that it would be an easier game for me. I could actually concentrate on playing a bit of hockey."

Boston games always brought on anxiety for Schultz. They were a team evenly matched in terms of toughness, with guys such as Wayne Cashman and most particularly, Terry O'Reilly. Schultz went toe-to-toe with O'Reilly at least eight times in his career and always said O'Reilly was the toughest guy he had fought in the league.

Despite his penalty history and penchant for pounding faces, Schultz was never suspended. Throughout his career, Schultz had many talks with league president Clarence Campbell about his antics on the ice, but Campbell was well aware of the power of the fighters to sell the game, and he rarely handed out suspensions to the league's dangerous guys.

Following the 1975–76 season, after getting swept out of the Stanley Cup finals by the Canadiens, Schultz was traded to the Los Angeles Kings. It was a difficult moment for the tough guy who had earned his reputation as a Flyer.

He played four more seasons with the Kings, the Pittsburgh Penguins and the Buffalo Sabres, never once straying from his combative style. Like many fighters in the league that attain Schultz-type status, their careers do not usually last long, and after 535 games, Schultz ended his reign in the NHL as the league's most dominant fighter when he retired in 1980 as a member of the Buffalo Sabres.

Tie Domi: Small Package, Powerful Punch

It seems only fitting that as Tie Domi was growing up in Belle River, Ontario, he loved to watch his favorite Toronto Maple Leafs player, Dave "Tiger" Williams. Tiger Williams was never a big hulking enforcer like Dave Schultz, but he had a combative nature and a wild streak that a young Tie, being on the diminutive side, could relate to.

However, as much as he admired Tiger Williams, Domi probably never envisioned he'd make it into the big leagues. Growing up in the small community of Belle River, near Windsor, Ontario, Tie, the youngest of three children, first began playing football and soccer. He often played with his older brothers and their friends on a local field, but despite the age and size differences, Tie competed alongside them, never letting any weaknesses show.

Tahir (Tie) Domi's parents, John and Meryem, were Albanian immigrants. They came to Canada in the 1950s after fleeing the repressive communist regime. During their escape, John Domi was shot just above his right eye and never had the bullet removed. He kept it as a reminder to himself and his family of the reasons why they moved to Canada and what it took for them to get there. Tie picked up on his father's lessons early on in life.

Perseverance and toughness were two traits young Tie Domi would need to break into the hockey world. At the start of his hockey career, Tie's height of 5 feet 7 inches did not matter all that much, but when he entered the junior ranks and tried to make his way through as a tough guy, he had to convince a lot of people that he could make it to the NHL.

"I had to fight my way into the league," Domi recalled. "They said I was too small to be a tough guy. So I had to beat those odds to just get a shot at the NHL."

In his first year playing for the Peterborough Petes of the Ontario Hockey League, Domi played in just 18 games but still managed to accumulate 79 penalty minutes. In his second season in 1987–88 with the Petes, he proved his naysayers wrong, playing in 60 games, scoring 22 goals, getting 21 assists and racking up 292 penalty minutes.

Domi's goal totals and pugnacious style caught the attention of the Toronto Maple Leafs, who chose him 27th overall at the 1988 NHL Draft, well ahead of other, more offensively minded players like Mark Recchi, Rob Blake, Joe Juneau and Alexander Mogilny.

After one year of conditioning with the Leafs' farm system, Domi finally made his NHL debut for the 1989–90 season. Naturally wanting to prove himself, he got into a fight and picked up 37 minutes in penalties in his first game. Detroit Red Wings coach Jacques Demers was so enraged with Domi's on-ice antics that the coach tried to leap over the glass separating the two benches to get at Leafs coach Doug Carpenter.

Despite Domi's big opening, the Leafs gave up on him after he had played just two games, trading him to the New York Rangers. Domi had more success with the Rangers, but that success also came with a heavy cost.

During a February 5, 1991, contest against state rival New York Islanders, Domi had one of the best games of his brief career, scoring the game-winning goal, getting an assist and winning two fights. Domi skated off the ice that night feeling like a champion, but then he was called into head coach Roger Neilson's office, and his life took a turn for the worse.

"I thought I was getting sent to the minors," Domi recalled. "[Neilson] said to me 'Your father passed away at nine o'clock tonight.' He'd seen part of the game; he was playing cards with his friends. I think he was probably pretty proud of me that night."

Domi held in his pain at the loss of his father and focused his energies on his work. Under the bright lights on Broadway, Domi began to add a little more showmanship to his game, often saluting the crowd after a fight, and he once rode his stick in honor of his boyhood hero Tiger Williams. Domi, though, developed his own signature move that defined his career.

On February 9, 1992, the New York Rangers played the Detroit Red Wings. Ever since joining the league, Domi's skills as a fighter stood in the shadow of big Bob Probert, reigning heavyweight of the NHL at that time. Domi had always been itching to get his shot at the title, and on that night, he finally got his chance about 10 minutes into the game when he and Probert squared off at center ice. Probert seemed up have the upper hand in the fight, but Domi managed to get in one good punch that caused a cut over Probert's eye.

The scuffle lasted nearly 30 seconds before the linesmen intervened, with Domi thinking he had won. He even had the nerve to make repeated hand gestures across his waist as if he was wearing the heavyweight championship belt. Although the Rangers fans loved it, the Red Wings players were not happy, and his antics led to an all-out brawl.

Bob Probert spoke of the incident in his biography *Tough Guy:* "He was saying to me, 'Come on,

Bob, Macho Man wants a shot at the title.' He called himself Macho Man, like the big time wrestler. I said, 'Ah, you little fucker, okay, come on!' He got lucky, when he grazed me, and I got cut just above the eye. He didn't really hit me, just wandered through with a left.... Later, the coach, Bryan Murray, asked me, 'What the fuck are you wasting your time with that little goofball Domi for? You've got nothing to prove.' 'Aw, fuck,' I said. 'I gave him a shot.'"

Despite lacking an obvious victory, Domi had made his mark in the NHL. The fight, however, left some people wanting a clearer idea of who was the reigning champion. Domi missed out on the two clubs' next meeting because of an injury, but he was front and center the following season on December 2, 1992, when the Wings and the Rangers played once again.

The day before the game, reporters kept asking Domi about Probert and whether he was aware of the hype building up toward the game. Domi knew what was expected of him once the opening puck dropped, and he was ready for it. The day of the game, *USA Today* and a New York tabloid ran a side-by-side comparison of Domi and Probert, with their stats, fight history and a likely outcome if they fought.

It was only 37 seconds into the game before Domi and Probert dropped their gloves. The fight had the crowd on its feet, cheering the two heavyweights. Probert got the best of the matchup, throwing what seemed like 30 to 40 punches, while Domi got in a few good shots of his own. The winner of the bout did not really matter because the fans ate up every moment. Domi received a $500 fine and a two-day suspension for hyping the fight in the media, something the NHL frowns upon. The league tolerated fighting but not staged fights.

A few games into the 1992–93 season, Domi was traded to the Winnipeg Jets. When reporters asked Rangers general manager Neil Smith why he sent Domi and fellow tough guy Kris King to the Jets, Smith explained that the game was changing and had less room for the fighters.

"There are a lot more skilled players in the game and a faster tempo. In all due respect to Tie, he couldn't get into our lineup. It's all well and good to be popular, but you've got to get into games."

It was a stinging criticism, but Domi had been forced to prove himself all his life and he was not about to change his approach to hockey now. Besides, Winnipeg welcomed him with open arms. The day before he joined the Jets, rookie star Teemu Selanne had a stick broken over his back in a game against the Minnesota North Stars. When Domi walked into the dressing room for the first time, Selanne gave him a big hug because he knew he would not have to put up with too many cheap shots anymore with an enforcer of Domi's stature on the club.

Critics often claim that the enforcer role does not work, saying that it is akin to fighting for peace. However, the arrival of Domi and King in Winnipeg helped Selanne establish a new NHL rookie record of 76 goals in a season. At the time of the Domi trade on December 28, Selanne had only scored 28 goals. From Domi's first game with the Jets to the end of the season, Selanne potted an incredible 46 goals, largely because the team's tough guys created extra room for Selanne.

Domi lasted only one full season with the Jets, racking up 347 penalty minutes in 81 games in 1993–94. He was traded back to the team that first drafted him—the Toronto Maple Leafs—near the end of the 1994–95 season.

Fighters rarely play more than 500 career games, and Domi wanted to be in the NHL for as long as possible, so he started to add new aspects to his game. Instead of being just another fighter, he took advantage of his strong skating to become an elite fore checker and a guy that could park himself in front of the opposing goaltender's net to screen a shot. This is not to say that Domi did not stop fighting; he even got into a few scraps when he wasn't on the ice.

On a night in between games in Chicago, Domi and a group of his fellow Leafs teammates decided to visit a local bar. A group of inebriated U.S. marines also in the bar thought it would be a good idea to harass a few of the Leafs players. Domi stepped in between the players and told them that the biggest of their group would be allowed one free punch and then Domi would be allowed to reply in kind. The biggest and dumbest of the marines stepped up.

"This guy hauls back and punches Tie in the face," one of Domi's teammates recalled, "and Tie looks at him and says, 'That's not your best shot, I'll give you one more.' Now, I can tell this guy has broken his hand and his buddies are like, 'It looks like we picked on the wrong midget.' He can't punch with his right hand, so he gives Tie a little baby punch with his left hand, and then Tie must have hit this guy 50 times. He was begging Tie to stop."

Of course, Domi had other famous incidents. In March 2001 when the Toronto Maple Leafs were visiting the Philadelphia Flyers, Domi was sent to the penalty box on a minor infraction. Domi was not a well-liked player in Philadelphia, and the fans that night sitting by the penalty box let Domi know it by tossing garbage at him.

"They threw stuff at me. Once was enough. After the second one, I told the guy in the penalty box that after one more I was going to squirt water. So I squirted water," Domi said after the game.

Domi used his water bottle to shower the front row of fans. Flyers fan Chris Falcone took exception to this. With his judgment likely clouded by a few beers, Falcone jumped from his second-row seat and landed on the glass separating the fans from the penalty box. Falcone tried to lean in and land a punch, but the glass gave way, and he fell right into the lion's den. Domi managed to get in a few good punches before linesman Kevin Collins jumped into the box to pull Domi off of Falcone. For the incident, Domi did not receive any additional penalties or punishment from the league. Falcone for his part received a large gash across his forehead and a trip to the hospital in the back of a police cruiser.

"You know it's all part of the game. It's nice to see the fans get involved, I guess," Domi said with a chuckle to reporters after the game.

As fun as it was to watch Domi's fighting spirit on the ice, his temper eventually got the best of him and cost his team dearly in the second round of the 2001 playoffs in game four of the Leafs series against the New Jersey Devils. With only seven seconds left in the game and Toronto leading 3–1, Domi elbowed Scott Niedermayer in the head, leaving the Jersey's star defenseman with a minor concussion. Domi was suspended for the rest of the series and—because Toronto lost in seven games—for the first eight games of the 2001–02 season as well.

Despite momentary lapses in judgment, Domi remained an integral part of the Leafs lineup, and on March 3, 2006, he celebrated a milestone not many enforcers or tough guys have achieved; he played in his 1000th career NHL game. Over the course of those 1000 games, Domi fought a total of 268 times.

"Pretty good for a guy who wasn't supposed to make it, eh?" said Domi to reporters before playing in that 1000th game.

At the end of that season, the Leafs opted to buy out his contract, and instead of searching for a team, Domi retired on his own terms. During his career, he played in 1020 games, scored 104 goals, had 141 assists and accumulated 3515 minutes in penalties, third overall on the all-time list, just 55 minutes shy of second-place Dale Hunter.

Other than pounding his way through to the heavyweight status in the NHL, Tie Domi also tried his hand at acting, appearing in the 1999 independent film, *Men of Means* and in *Mystery, Alaska* as himself. He also played a full season in the Canadian International Soccer League during the summer of 1995 as well as appearing in two pre-season exhibition games as a place kicker for the Toronto Argonauts in the Canadian Football League.

Chris Nilan: Boston Tough

Chris "Knuckles" Nilan is the true stereotypical picture of the hockey fighter. All the elements of a Hollywood script are present in his life: he grew up in a rough neighborhood, got into street fights every weekend, had the "me-against-the-world" attitude as well as the fearlessness in fighting anyone just to prove he could, and finally, a ticket to the big leagues when all doubted him.

Nilan overcame adversity during his life, and he not only played in the NHL but also thrived in Montreal alongside Bob Gainey and Guy Carbonneau to win a Stanley Cup in 1986. These achievements seemed impossible for Nilan as a kid growing up in Boston's West Roxbury neighborhood.

Nilan spent his childhood days idolizing the great Boston Bruins of the 1970s led, of course, by Phil Esposito and Bobby Orr. Before the great era of Orr and the two Stanley Cup victories, hockey was not all that popular in Boston after the franchise spent so many years without a championship win. As a result, there were few rinks around the city for kids to practice on, and because of this, Nilan's first time on skates at the age of five was on a frozen puddle in a parking lot near his house. Nilan got into hockey just as Boston exploded with hockey fever, and rinks began to sprout across the city.

But as much as he began to love the game, Nilan was constantly distracted by his other talent—finding trouble. "As a kid growing up in Boston, I fought a lot in the streets; I was constantly getting in fights. I just never backed down from anybody," Nilan recalled. "It was the type of neighborhood where if you let people push you around, you'd get pushed around."

An incident like that occurred one summer when he was sitting on a curb with his friend outside a local restaurant. A car pulled up, and young guys got out and started making fun of Nilan's haircut on their way into the building. Once the guys were inside the building, Nilan took out the knife he always carried with him and slashed all the tires on the car. Nilan and his friend took off, but a few days later, the same guys returned and gave Nilan and his friend a good beating.

Like Tie Domi, Nilan was not the most physically imposing of hockey players, so he had to make up for his lack of size with sheer determination. In his early days on the ice, Nilan was not known as a fighter, mostly because fighting was

not allowed in the lower ranks, but once he grad-
uated to the tougher leagues, Nilan followed
a "take-no-prisoners" attitude.

Early on in his hockey career, it didn't look as
though Nilan would go anywhere, but his minor
league coach Paul King introduced him to former
Boston Bruins tough guy Fernie Flaman, who
was coaching the hockey team at Northeastern
University. After seeing the determination in
Nilan's game, Flaman offered him a scholarship.
But Nilan was anything but impressive at Northeastern, playing only a minor role on the hockey
team, potting just 17 points in 20 games.

The summer of 1978 was Nilan's NHL draft
year, and despite his lack of success with Northeastern, he was doggedly certain that one team
would take a chance on him. Weeks before the
draft, his old coach Paul King called up his friend
Montreal Canadiens legend Dickie Moore and
asked him to relay a message to the Canadiens
brass to send someone to see Nilan play. The Canadiens, like the other teams, were unimpressed
with Nilan but drafted him 231st overall with
their last pick; it was more as a favor to King than
anything Nilan did to deserve the draft pick.

Nilan spent one more year at Northwestern
then traveled to Montreal for his first training
camp in the fall of 1979. He played the scrim-
mage games with all his heart and dropped his

gloves every chance he got, but he didn't make the team; he was sent to Montreal's farm team in the American Hockey League, the Nova Scotia Voyageurs. He sat out a few of the first games of the season, but Nilan finally got his shot in a game against the Maine Mariners, and in his first shift, he got into a fight with the reigning champion of the league. Nilan made short work of the guy and the rest of the challengers that season. Seeing his progress in the minors, the Canadiens decided they could use a little toughness and called Nilan up half way through the 1979–80 season.

After getting his feet wet in his first game in the NHL against the Atlanta Flames, Nilan was ready to drop the gloves in his second game, this time against the Philadelphia Flyers Bob "Hound Dog" Kelly.

"I put him down, and that was it," Nilan said.

With that fight, the tough kid from Boston made a place for himself with the Canadiens organization, finishing out the season and a few games in the playoffs before the Canadiens were eliminated.

Over the next three seasons, not wanting to lose his spot on the team, Nilan instigated fights and dropped his gloves almost every time he stepped out onto the ice. However, this was all he was being used for, hardly ever getting time out for a regular shift. Head coach Bob Berry often scratched Nilan for the home games and left him with only five minutes of ice time per game. It became so frustrating for Nilan that he walked into the general manager's office to demand a trade. Luckily, though, by the 1983–84 season, the Canadiens had hired Jacques Lemaire as head coach, and he envisioned a greater role for Nilan than just a fighter.

Lemaire's first decision as coach was to move Nilan from the fourth line up to the top defensive line with Bob Gainey and Guy Carbonneau. Over the next three years, the trio worked hard to become one of the top defensive lines in the NHL. After his first full season in 1984–85 with the Gainey and Carbonneau, Nilan proved that he could score a few goals as well as use his fists, getting a career-high 21 goals and 16 assists. He also piled up a Canadiens' record of 358 penalty minutes. Despite the success, Nilan always had someone reminding him of his role.

"Jacques Lemaire basically told me, 'Don't go start thinking you're a goal-scorer now,'" Nilan recounted.

Then before the 1985–86 season, Lemaire stepped down as coach and was replaced by Jean Perron. The Canadiens were a team looking for an identity that year, with a mix of aging veterans and up-and-coming rookies. Nilan's year got off to a rough start when the Canadiens played the Boston Bruins. Although he was from Boston, Nilan was never one to give any team an easy time, and in the course of the game, he received a rare 10-minute penalty (resulting in a 10-minute power play) for butt-ending Bruins forward Rick Middleton in the face. Nilan protested the call, claiming to have just smacked Middleton in the face with his glove, but the referee saw it differently, and so did the league, which handed him a 10-game suspension for the infraction.

The boy from Boston was suddenly enemy number one in his hometown as newspaper articles and radio call-in shows publicly criticized Nilan as a dirty player. Once he was back from suspension, however, Nilan returned to the ice and continued to fight.

The Canadiens finished out the 1985–86 season in good standing and made it into the playoffs. No one expected Montreal to go far with their team of rookies and aging veterans, but the Canadiens surprised everyone by winning the Stanley Cup. Nilan had made sure the Canadiens rookies were protected, racking up 141 minutes in penalties. The fighting, however, took him out of the final games of the Stanley Cup series against Calgary when he injured ligaments in his ankle as a result of a fight with the Flames Neil Sheehy.

After the Canadiens dream season, Nilan's relationship with head coach Jean Perron deteriorated to the point that midway through the 1987–88 season, Nilan once again asked for a trade. This time he got his wish and was traded to the New York Rangers in exchange for draft picks.

But Nilan was never the same after leaving the Canadiens, playing no more than 40 games per season for the Rangers before another trade sent him to the Boston Bruins, where he began to see his career coming to an end. He no longer fought with the same enthusiasm, and he had lost the drive to succeed that he had possessed in the early days. In the middle of the 1991–92 season, the Bruins placed Nilan on waivers, and he was picked up by the Montreal Canadiens. Nilan played just 17 games with the Canadiens that season and seven playoff games before retiring as a member of the Montreal Canadiens after 13 years in the NHL.

After the games were over and the lights were turned off, Nilan embarked on the most difficult fight of his life—the one against drugs and alcohol. Over the course of his career, Nilan had been in close to 300 fights, recorded 3574 penalty minutes and undergone a whopping 30 surgical procedures, which left him in constant pain. For years he had been using OxyContin and Percocet to relieve the pain, but when he stopped playing hockey, he continued to use, then abuse, the drugs. Then came the alcohol abuse on top of it. Had it not been for his girlfriend, who forced him to get the necessary help to conquer the battle, he might have ended up like other fighters Derek Boogaard and Wade Belak.

"I don't want to go back to this miserable life," Nilan said. "It's a fight, but I am vigilant. This is the fight of my life, and I will win."

Chris Nilan was the fastest player in NHL history to reach 3000 career penalty minutes, and his average of 4.42 minutes per game is the highest among players with at least 2500 career penalty minutes. Only Shane Churla (1986–97) bested his average per game total with 4.72 minutes per game, having played in 488 games and recoding 2301 total career penalty minutes. Chris Nilan spent so much time in the penalty box, most of it playing for the Montreal Canadiens, that when the Montreal Forum was being dismantled, Nilan purchased the penalty box.

Tony Twist: The Toughest

People remember Bob Probert as a fighter and Dave "The Hammer" Schultz as a mean enforcer, but Tony Twist is not on many people's minds when they think of hockey enforcers. However, any player who has ever fought Twist surely can never forget the man because he was one of the toughest enforcers in the NHL.

Twist was reputed to deliver one of the hardest punches in the league during his 10 seasons with the St. Louis Blues and Quebec Nordiques, and once that reputation was set, fighters across the league were a little scared of going up against him.

In addition to his size (256 pounds and 6-foot-1) and strength, Twist brought the art of enforcing to a whole new level. Unlike some tough guys who like to think of themselves as two-way players able to contribute, Twist knew he was in the NHL for one reason only and that if he stopped fighting, he would no longer have a job. Twist's approach was not just to fight when called upon; he made fighting an educational pursuit. Before each game, he scouted his future opponents and watched hours of videos on the tough guys in the league.

On top of mental preparation, Twist religiously primed his body for the rigors of fighting. His most important ritual was to toughen up his knuckles by punching a concrete floor over and over for about 15 minutes a night while he watched TV. The constant pounding conditioned his fists to recover from a fight, so if he was involved in a fight in the first period, his knuckles would be ready for another fight in the second, sometimes sooner. This conditioning made him a devastating fighter; he knew how his opponents fought, and he could hit them with fists of concrete.

"It really helped my career, I promise you that," Twist said, speaking of that particular concrete-punching ritual. "If you fight 33 times in a year, I don't care who you are, if you don't toughen your knuckles up, you're not going to be able to perform."

Being tough and working hard were the lessons Twist learned early in life in Prince George, British Columbia. His grandfather was an accomplished boxer and winner of Canadian welterweight titles. Twist's father was a different kind of tough, serving 32 years with the Royal Canadian Mounted Police.

Twist began his hockey career at the age of four, and by the time he was 16, he was playing for the Junior A Prince George Spruce Kings. He had already evolved into a fighter.

"At 16 years old, I found I could fight, and I enjoyed it," said Twist.

While playing with the Spruce Kings, Twist fought in almost every game, making him a fan favorite. But despite his fan support, Twist was less than hopeful about his prospects of making the NHL when he came up for the draft in 1988. In his final two years of junior in the Western Hockey League with the Saskatoon Blades, Twist had only one goal in 119 games. However, it was his 407 minutes in penalties during that time that caught the eye of the St. Louis Blues, who selected the hulking winger 177th overall in the ninth round of the draft.

At the Blues training camp, Twist was not the only rookie enforcer the Blues were looking at. He decided that in order to get the club's attention, he had to challenge the guys going for his job. With every shift during training camp, Twist took on all challengers and proved he was ready for the majors. But the Blues management thought differently and passed on Twist's services, sending him to the Peoria Rivermen of the International Hockey League for the 1988–89 season. There he accumulated 312 minutes in penalties.

Back in the NHL, the Blues' resident tough guy Todd Ewen was suspended near the end of the season, which would carry over to the next year. Since the team was without an enforcer to start the year, Twist finally got his call up to the league for the 1989–90 season.

On his second or third shift in his first NHL game played at the old Chicago Stadium against the Blackhawks, Twist squared off against the Hawks' top enforcer, Wayne Van Dorp. The fight didn't last long as Twist violently rained down punches on the completely overwhelmed Chicago tough guy. Twist's style was to come out fast and hard. There was no dancing around or looking for an opening. A fight with Tony Twist was on from the moment the gloves dropped. Even when his opponent turned his face away from the blows and Twist was punching the back of his helmet, he never stopped swinging until either the linesmen jumped in or his target was down.

Twist remained in the NHL for 48 games that season, and though he played in only 28 of them, he managed to send a clear message to the other enforcers in the league that a new sheriff was in town. In the 28 games he played, Twist was involved in 21 fights.

Twist finished the season out with the Blues but was shipped back to the Peoria Rivermen. After one more season in the IHL, Twist was traded to the Quebec Nordiques late in the 1990–91 season. Quebec at that time was one of the youngest teams in the NHL, featuring such future stars as Joe Sakic, Mats Sundin and Owen Nolan. Nordiques head coach Pierre Page gave Twist plenty of ice time to protect these new stars. Twist was not only popular with Page but also with Quebec fans, who were suffering through a horrible season. Although Twist's mother was French Canadian, he had never learned the language when growing up. However, by the end of that year, he was able to comfortably conduct post-game interviews in French, further endearing him to local fans.

Searching through videos of Twist on You-Tube, I could not find a single fight of Twist where he clearly lost. There were a few draws when the linesmen jumped in, but they saved Twist's opponents from getting hurt rather than the other way round.

Over three seasons with the Nordiques, Twist firmly established himself as the toughest tough guy in the NHL, and no one wanted to mess with him. But the title also brought a problem. The main role of an enforcer is to make opposing players think twice before taking liberties with the team's top players. The Nordiques did not even have to play Twist—just seeing him on the bench was threat enough for their opponents; knowing that they would see him in the next game kept the goons of the league in check, leaving room for top players such as Sakic and Sundin to work their magic.

Twist's career stats are not padded with penalty minutes like other enforcers in the league who had a similar number of career games because he just did not have to fight often. Over his 10-year career in the NHL, Twist accumulated only 1121 penalty minutes in 445 games, about an average of 2.5 minutes per game; lower statistics not normally seen for the top NHL fighters. Tigers Williams, for example, played in 962 games and accumulated 3966 penalty minutes, which works out to an average of 4.1 minutes per game, while Chris Nilan averaged 4.4 penalty minutes per game.

"I don't think you need to fight every game to do your job," said Twist. "It just came down to the intimidation factor. I was able to perform my job, but that's not to say I didn't want to fight. There were a bunch of times I went out looking for them, but I just wasn't able to get them."

After punching up in Quebec, Twist was traded back to the St. Louis Blues for the 1994–95 lock-out-shortened season. Over the next four years, Twist had a few challengers to his heavyweight title, but none were as entertaining as his bouts with Bob Probert. Probert, a Chicago Blackhawk, represented a huge contrast in fighting style from Twist. The Hawks brawler preferred to tire his opponents out before unleashing a barrage of lethal punches, whereas Twist was a surgical power striker. The two heavyweights fought several times in their careers, but in all the fights, neither could be definitively declared the winner.

"I wanted to knock your head off and kill you, and [Probert] wanted to tire you out then beat the [daylights] out of you," said Twist.

After the 1998–99 season, Twist entered into free agency and parted ways with the Blues. He was in the middle of contract talks with the

Philadelphia Flyers when his career was derailed after he got into a nasty motorcycle accident in St. Louis. He had been driving down a street when a car suddenly pulled out in front of his bike. Twist hit the car, flipping over the handlebars and landing on his feet (this is not a lie or an embellishment) about 55 feet away, then skidded on his boots for another 20 feet.

"I skidded like Fred Flintstone," said Twist about the accident. "The impact was so hard that I wound up with no jeans on, no underwear, nothing. When I went over the handlebars, they grabbed a little bit of my jeans and ripped them completely off. It broke my three-inch leather belt, and I flipped just once. It was incredible, I don't know how I survived it."

As a result of the initial impact, Twist's pelvis was fractured and he suffered a severe injury to his left knee. The accident put an end to his NHL career but did not affect his fighting nature.

In the Spawn comic book series, creator Todd McFarlane named a mob character Antonio "Tony Twist" Twistelli. The former hockey player did not take kindly to having his name used in such a manner and sued McFarlane for $25 million for profiting from his name. The lawsuit was launched in 1998, but it wasn't until 2004 that Twist was awarded $15 million by a St. Louis court. McFarlane appealed, and the two settled out of court for $5 million.

Twist finished his career having played 445 games, scored only 10 goals, having 18 assists with 1121 penalty minutes.

Bob Probert: A Fighter's Fighter

When one thinks of an enforcer, Bob Probert is usually at the top of the list. For 16 seasons Bob Probert was the poster child for NHL enforcers. From 1985 to 2002, playing for the Detroit Red Wings and the Chicago Blackhawks, Probert was the man the opposing team had to answer to if they got out of hand, and he haunted the dreams of lesser fighters who knew that at some point, they would have to face his fists of fury.

However, Probert was also the perfect example of the darker side of fighting in hockey; he sought solace in alcohol and drugs to escape from the pain and pressure of the big leagues. It is a problem that has plagued fighters for generations but only truly came to light in the public battles that Probert experienced.

A fact often lost in the talk of his battle with drugs and his many fights on the ice was that Probert was a good hockey player. From his early days playing in his hometown of Windsor, Ontario, Probert was a goal-scoring forward before he discovered his other hockey talent. Playing for the Windsor Club 240 in a minor league, Probert scored 60 goals in 55 games and had only 40 minutes in penalties. It wasn't until he hit his growth spurt and went into his first season of junior hockey with the Brantford Alexanders of the Ontario Hockey League that he truly embraced the role of enforcer, accumulating 133 penalty minutes as a 17-year-old rookie. His toughness and ability to score goals prompted the Detroit Red Wings to select Probert 46th overall in the 1983 NHL Entry Draft.

It was clear from the draft that the Red Wings were going for toughness at that draft, signing Joey Kocur and Stu Grimson. Someone was going to have to protect their number one selection that year, a young Steve Yzerman. After a few years of conditioning in the OHL and the AHL, Probert finally got called up to the Wings about halfway through the 1985–86 season. He immediately displayed his skill at the game, scoring 8 goals with 13 assists for 21 points in 44 games in his rookie year, but he also showed the Motor City fans that he could punch it up with the best in the league.

Probert's first NHL fight came on November 11, 1985, when the Wings faced off against the Vancouver Canucks. Playing in only his 12th career game was Canucks rookie enforcer Craig

Coxe. Both players were looking to prove something. The ensuing fight that night in Vancouver has gone down in NHL lore, equaled only by the rematch in the 1986–87 season.

The first fight featured a flurry of right-handed haymakers by Coxe that seemed to take Probert out of the fight. But after pushing Coxe up against the boards, Probert came back with a flurry of his own punches and knocked Coxe to the ice with a hard right to the side of the face. It was a classic hockey punch up, with both players trading punishing hits to the face until one fell. The fight lasted 40 seconds.

Their second bout was featured in one of Don Cherry's famous *Rock 'Em Sock 'Em* videos. Cherry counted 71 punches between the two players in a 50-second fight in which Probert landed two nasty upper cuts to Coxe's face before linesmen interrupted the battle. Cherry could hardly contain his glee over the battle. Highlights of the fight spread across the news on November 19, 1987, cementing Probert's status as one of the NHL's new elite enforcers.

After a brief return to the AHL, Probert returned to the Red Wings for the 1986–87 season and never again looked back from the NHL. That year, he scored 13 goals and recorded 11 assists in 63 games as well as piling up 221 minutes in penalties. Things only got better for the 1987–88 campaign when Probert had the best season of his career playing on Steve Yzerman's right wing. Probert finished with 29 goals and 33 assists, and he somehow managed to do that while sitting in the sin bin for 398 minutes. He was also called out to play in the All-Star game. His combination of fighting talent with scoring skill had not been seen in the NHL since the days of John Ferguson in the 1960s.

"He's a really good guy in addition to being one of the toughest guys around," said fellow tough guy Chris Simon. "You look at what he did when he had 29 goals and 398 penalty minutes. I mean, I don't think you'll ever see that happen again."

Probert was all business on the ice, and his main job in those early years on the line with Steve Yzerman was to protect his captain. Anyone who took liberties with Yzerman had to answer to Probert. Not many were foolish enough, but every once in a while, a player would forget just who was the sheriff in town.

For example, an incident occurred during a game between the Buffalo Sabres and the Detroit Red Wings on December 23, 1987. After a scrum, Yzerman got involved with the much larger and tougher Kevin Maguire. Yzerman was hopelessly out-muscled, receiving several punches to the face. Probert, who was about to be escorted off to the penalty box for a previous minor infraction, saw his captain in trouble, threw the linesman aside and made a beeline to help him. A pile-up of players prevented Probert from getting at Maguire, so he circled the bodies like a shark waiting for his moment to strike against the player who dared touch Yzerman. Buffalo goaltender Tom Barrasso saw Probert waiting to lash out and tried to stop him but instead got his mask punched off his face as well as another right to the jaw. Buffalo defenseman Phil Housley also tried to step in front, but one look from Probert sent him fleeing. Probert only had eyes for number 19, Maguire, but two linesmen were blocking the way, trying to separate Yzerman from Maguire while also keeping Maguire from getting killed by Probert. Unable to stand up toe to toe with Maguire, Probert got his revenge by sucker punching him as he was being held up by the referee.

"He was tough as nails. The fights from his early days were scary to watch," said tough guy Peter Worrell.

But with instant success for young guy in his early 20s, a lot of problems can rise to the surface. From his rookie year to 1989, Probert was arrested several times for driving under the influence of alcohol, and he went in and out of rehab throughout the early years of his career with Detroit. His behavior became so unpredictable that Red Wings management assigned assistant coach Colin Campbell the job of keeping Probert out of trouble. Probert was so adept at pushing Campbell's buttons—even giving him the nickname "Soupy," after Campbell's Soup—that he challenged him to a boxing match in the Red Wings dressing room.

"Soupy had played for the Penguins, Oilers, Canucks, and Wings and had done a little bit of boxing back then. But he was about ten years older than me," Probert wrote in his book *Tough Guy*, which was published posthumously. "So we went down to the dressing room, moved the benches, put the gloves on and had three one-minute rounds. At the start of each round, I'd drill him in the head and he'd try to paste his forehead on my chest. The next day at the game Soupy had two black eyes...."

As harmless as Probert thought his antics were, the partying eventually caught up to him on March 2, 1989, when he was caught at the border crossing between Detroit and Windsor with 14.3 grams of cocaine in his underwear. He was given a three-month stay at the Federal Medical Center in Rochester, Minnesota, followed up with another three months in a halfway house. He was suspended indefinitely from the NHL.

After serving out his sentence, Probert received a temporary work permit from the U.S. Government, and the NHL lifted his ban in March 1990.

However, because of his attempt to enter into the United States with cocaine, the U.S. Immigration Department did not allow him to leave the country, even to play games in Canada. He played his first game back in Canada against the Toronto Maple Leafs in December 1992. It had been four years since his previous visit to his home country.

After his release from rehab and return to playing form, Probert continued where he left off in the league, scoring 20 goals with 24 assists and 276 minutes in penalties in 63 games during the 1991–92 season. Life was returning to normal for Probert, and he was more than proud of his accomplishment of kicking drugs and booze, and he was hoping to build a solid foundation for a sober life. But addiction does not let its victims go easily, and once more Probert was back in the news on July 15, 1994, when he crashed his motorcycle in a Detroit suburb. Not only did he have three times the blood alcohol limit, but the police also found cocaine in his system. The Red Wings had had enough, and just four days after the accident, they put him on waivers.

Probert was again given a chance, but this time by the Chicago Blackhawks, division rivals of the Red Wings. Probert missed the entire 1994–95 lockout-shortened season recovering from his injuries and going through substance abuse treatment. When he returned to hockey with his new club, he was up to his old fighting ways. In his first game against the Edmonton Oilers in the 1995–96 season, he was thrown out for instigating a fight.

Probert, however, did enjoy a renewed sense of purpose with the Hawks, scoring 19 goals with 21 assists and 237 penalty minutes in 78 games. Off the ice, Probert was managing to get his life back together as well. Blackhawks management began to loosen the reins they had on him and roomed him with some of the young players on the road so they could benefit from the hard lessons Probert had learned in the league.

Probert played seven seasons with Chicago without any major incident, just the normal punch-ups and bloody jerseys. But along the way, he also achieved a few career milestones.

On February 13, 1999, he scored the last goal ever in Toronto's famed Maple Leafs Gardens. In attendance that day was 90-year-old Harold "Mush" March, who scored the first goal at the Gardens, also for the Blackhawks on November 12, 1931. In 2000 Probert became just the sixth NHL player to pass the 3000-penalty mark. However, by the start of the 2002–03 season, he was no longer the same player he used to be. The years of drug and alcohol abuse on top of his role as an enforcer had slowed him down considerably, so he bowed out of the league. He immediately took a job with the Blackhawks broadcast team, providing colorful commentary as only he could.

"It's not easy, but it's exciting to step into something else in the game instead of not doing anything," Probert said at the time.

With his retirement, reporters from every city asked the resident enforcers for a few words on Probert's career. All had good things to say, even the players he had beaten up.

"In my mind, he's the greatest fighter of all time," said enforcer Georges Laraque. "To last as long as he did with all the young guns coming in, trying to make a name for themselves by fighting him...he's almost 40 and he never turned anybody down. He's the all-time warrior."

"He had a long career. I'm glad I'm not him. If you were waiting to prove yourself as a tough guy, you had to prove it with Probie. Now there's no legitimate number one guy," said Peter Worrell.

Once the hectic pace of his NHL life ended, Probert had trouble adjusting to the lack of excitement and returned to his old habits. In 2003 he re-entered rehab for alcoholism and finally conquered his demons, focusing his energies on his wife and four kids. In between, he visited the Canadian troops in Afghanistan; had a cameo appearance in the Mike Myers film,

The Love Guru; and participated in the CBC television series, the *Battle of the Blades,* in which former hockey players were paired with figure skating champions in a competition for charity (Probert was the first eliminated).

Living life in the fast lane for several years eventually caught up with Probert. On July 5, 2010, while boating on Lake St. Clair near his home with his wife and kids, Probert collapsed and died of a massive heart attack at the age of 44. After his autopsy, it was discovered that he had been suffering from chronic traumatic encephalopathy, a degenerative brain disease.

Steve Yzerman remembered Probert in the forward of *Tough Guy*:

Fans may remember him for his fighting ability and goal scoring, but he was much more than that. Bob knew how to play the game. He was an intelligent player with great hockey sense. For a player with fists of stone, he had incredibly soft hands.... Hidden behind Bob's self-deprecating humor was a man who truly cared. He was grateful and loyal to people who treated him with respect. He was a rugged hockey player and an unselfish teammate willing to do anything for his team. He had a kind heart and a gentle soul.

"How do I want to be remembered?" Probert said when he announced his retirement. "I guess just as a hard-nosed player who played hard every night, gave it his all, got some points and got in some scraps."

John Kordic: The Tortured Soul

John "Rambo" Kordic's brief career in the NHL spanned seven seasons with four teams from 1985 to 1992. He was a pure fighter who only scored a career-high nine goals in one season. He played only in 244 NHL games, but for that brief period he was one of the most feared enforcers in the league. However, like many other tough guys, his life was surrounded by darkness and shrouded in tragedy.

Kordic was a wild fighter, hence the nickname "Rambo." He could fight equally well with both his left and right hands, making him tough to handle. But as tough as he was to fight on the ice, he was tougher off the ice when he began his descent into the world of drugs and alcohol.

Born in Edmonton, Alberta, on March 22, 1965, John Kordic dreamed of playing in the NHL and wanted to take after his idol Bobby Orr. As with other enforcers, Kordic started out in the sport as a goal scorer, able to out-muscle and push guys off the puck in order to get better opportunities at the net. But as the other kids caught up to him in size and out-passed him in talent, Kordic began to use only his size out on the ice.

"He could play," said his mother, Regina Kordic. "But something went wrong. He started using nothing but his fists. After a while, I didn't recognize my kid. I didn't raise him that way."

His fists, though, were highly prized in hockey, and Kordic pounded his way up the ranks, making the Western Hockey League with the Portland Winter Hawks in 1982–83. That season turned out pretty good for the fighter, winning the Memorial Cup with Portland. During the Entry Draft, Montreal Canadiens used their fourth-round selection to add some toughness to their team by choosing Kordic.

But the Canadiens left Kordic languishing in the WHL, and then the AHL with the Sherbrooke Canadiens for four years. It looked like he would never get the chance to show what he could do because the Canadiens already had tough guy Chris Nilan patrolling the ice for them. It was late in the 1985–86 season when Kordic finally got the call up to the big leagues. With just five games left in the season, the Canadiens were preparing to make their push into the playoffs and wanted to add a little more grit to their relatively young and small team. Kordic played 18 games in the playoffs that year, totaled 53 minutes in penalties and won a Stanley Cup.

"He beat the shit out of everybody," said Jean Perron, Montreal's coach at the time and now a Quebec City radio personality. "He was the best fighter in the league. Nobody could take John Kordic. The fans in the Forum would chant his name. Kor-dic! Kor-dic! Kor-dic!"

After another brief stint with the Canadiens farm team, Kordic was back with Montreal for the 1986–87 and quickly became a fan favorite. With that fame however, came the nightly pressures to perform, and like many fighters, the push to drop the gloves became difficult to handle. On one hand, a fighter embraces the crowd's cheers and relishes the high of the moment, but on the other hand, the nightly requirements of getting into a fight can wear the player down mentally. Kordic started coming apart early on.

His parents would watch the games and see their son in a battle in every game he played, which didn't help Kordic. "That really got to him," Perron said. "I remember seeing John crying into the phone after a game that we had won. I asked him what was wrong, and he said, 'My dad just gave me a hard time because I got into a fight tonight.'"

Kordic was a fan of telling his teammates and his coaches that he did not like to fight, but when he was on the ice, it was clear that he relished his role. But the pressure of fighting nightly is often too much for some players to handle. It wasn't long after signing a two-year deal with the Canadiens that Kordic began experimenting with cocaine and steroids. The city of Montreal had one of the best nightclub scenes, and Kordic stayed out until all hours drinking heavily, often missing team curfew and showing up late for practices.

However, as long as Kordic kept dropping the gloves, both the league and the Canadiens were willing to look the other way. Back then, if a player was caught using marijuana or cocaine, the league might issue a suspension, but Kordic was also pumping himself full of steroids, something that the league was willing to overlook.

Just before his contract with the Canadiens ended, Kordic was traded to the Toronto Maple Leafs in return for Russ Courtnall. But life in Toronto was less than perfect for Kordic. After the much-maligned trade, the Toronto media made Kordic the target of their aggression as they watched Courtnall flourish with the Canadiens. The negative media glare bothered Kordic, and it began to show when, during a game on December 14, 1988, he broke his stick over Edmonton Oilers forward Keith Acton. He received a 10-game suspension.

"While he was serving that suspension," said Gord Stellick, then general manager of the Leafs and now a broadcaster in Toronto, "I got tipped

off by a senior member of the Metro police that
I'd better tell John Kordic to watch out. I was told
that he was hanging around with hookers and
druggies and that he was getting into trouble.
I called him into the office and told him that, but
he denied it."

Through all his trials and tribulations in the
NHL, Kordic had always relied on his father to
keep him grounded in reality. Kordic called his
father after games to get his opinion, hear
his criticism or just to talk. But when his father
died of liver cancer in 1989, the enforcer's drug
and steroid abuse quickly began to spiral out of
control. The Toronto Maple Leafs management
was not sure what to do with him; they tried
sending Kordic to the minors and keeping him in
the press box, but the enforcer just descended
further into the mire of substance abuse.

Kordic began to ask the Leafs for advances on
his salary, and his teammates noticed a change,
jokingly calling him "Sniffy," referring to his
cocaine habit. The team even tried to enter him
into a rehab program, but Kordic did not want to
stop using. Drugs had become a way of life
for him.

In February 1991, the Leafs traded Kordic to
the Washington Capitals in exchange for a draft
pick. He only played seven games for the Capitals,
twice getting suspended by the club for what was

described as alcohol-related offenses. Unable to control him, the Capitals also gave up on Kordic.

With nowhere left to turn, Kordic was prompted by a former rehab clinic companion and Quebec defenseman Bryan Fogarty that he should ask the Nordiques for a position. Kordic's reputation had already spread across the league, and Quebec was his last hope.

"It wasn't something we were crazy about doing," said Nordiques head coach Pierre Pagé, "but we decided to take the risk."

There was one condition on his signing. If he was caught with and drugs or alcohol in his system, the team would immediately let him go, and he would likely never play in the NHL again. Kordic played just 19 games during the 1991–92 season with Quebec before once again relapsing.

"He came to me and cried. I said, 'Isn't that the deal we made?'" said Pagé. "We gave you a chance when no one else would, and I'm glad we did it. I'm still glad we did it."

Kordic spent his time in Quebec, as he had done in Montreal, visiting the city's seedy bars and strip clubs. It was in one of those strip clubs where Kordic fell in love with a stripper named Massé. But love still did not calm the darkness within, as he was then arrested for domestic assault on the young woman.

In the meantime, Kordic found work with the Cape Breton Oilers of the American Hockey League, but he lasted only 12 games. The Oilers could sense something was wrong with Kordic because he completely disregarded his duties on ice and constantly got into fights even when it didn't benefit the club. In the 12 games he played, he accumulated 141 minutes in penalties.

The offseason was the most difficult for Kordic. Without hockey, he spent much of his time in bars and strip clubs getting into fights and getting high.

On August 8, 1992, Kordic showed up at Motel Maxim in Quebec City, bruised and bloodied. He paid for a room, and a few hours later, he made abusive phone calls from his room and broke furniture. Police were called in, and it took seven cops to subdue the former NHL enforcer. Kordic was placed in an ambulance, and on the way to the hospital, he passed out and could not be revived. The autopsy revealed that he had died from lung failure as the result of heart malfunction caused by a lethal mix of alcohol, steroids and cocaine. He was just 27. It was a terrible and sad end to a career and a person who needed help.

Kordic played 244 NHL games, scored 17 goals, had 18 assists and accumulated 997 penalty minutes.

Derek Boogaard: The Boogey Man

The life of a tough guy is probably the hardest job in the NHL. If a player is not mentally strong enough to assume the role, the pressure can end up consuming him, and that's just what happened to Derek Boogaard.

Off the ice, teammates said Boogaard was the nicest, calmest person they knew, but when challenged to drop the gloves, he punished his opponents with impunity.

As a kid growing up in Saskatoon, Saskatchewan, he was a rather shy, awkward child who had a growth spurt sooner than the rest of the kids his age, so that by the time he was 15, he was 6-foot-3 and weighed 209 pounds. His clumsiness, his shyness and the fact that his father was an RCMP officer made him the target of verbal abuse by many of his classmates. A few of his peers were foolish enough to try to fight him, but Boogaard ended the fights quickly.

Encouraged by his parents to play hockey as an outlet for his daily frustrations as a teenager, Boogaard found that his size made him the center of positive attention on the ice, and he fell in love with the game. The player he grew up idolizing was fellow Saskatchewan native Wendel Clark of the Toronto Maple Leafs. Boogaard admired Clark's grit and energy on the ice and wanted to play just like him. However, because of his large size, Boogaard was often relied upon by his teammates to take on the role of an enforcer. He did not get into fights on the ice, but a gentle push into the boards by tall Boogaard on a kid much smaller often was enough to get the message across. Other parents often complained that he was simply too large to play against kids his same age. Despite the negative attention he received because of his size, it would play to his advantage when he joined the Melfort Mustangs of the Saskatchewan Junior Hockey League (SJHL).

In general, Boogaard was a calm player who only used his size when he needed to, but on several occasions in the early years, he lost his temper. One night, while playing for the Melfort Mustangs, something happened on the ice or an opposing player said something Boogaard didn't like, and he jumped into the opposing bench and began beating any player who came near him.

"He had gone ballistic," said his father of the incident. "It was something I hadn't seen before."

Boogaard was ejected from the game and was likely facing a long suspension when fate intervened and changed his life. In attendance that night were scouts from the Regina Pats of the Western Hockey League, who were impressed by Boogaard's passion for the game. That same night, the scouts offered him a chance to play for their club. Boogaard didn't know what job he was being recruited for, but it would bring him that much closer to his dream of landing a job in the NHL.

Things, however, did not get off to a good start. The Regina Pats had brought him on board for his physical toughness, and when he backed out of his first fight, he was demoted to the club's SJHL affiliate. He played with the club most of the 1998–99 season but never got much ice time. Near the end of the season, rather than ride the bench, Boogaard quit the team and returned home. But the Regina Pats could not resist Boogaard's potential as an enforcer. He had reached his full height of 6-foot-5, and so they called him back up to the Western Hockey League. However, he played in only five games before he was traded to the Prince George Cougars after losing a fight.

Clearly, the Regina Pats were not willing to give him any room to grow. With the Cougars, it seemed Boogaard had finally found a comfortable place to play. But luck was not on his side when late in the season he suffered a broken jaw in a fight. He considered giving up his dream of making it to the NHL and thought of quitting hockey for good, but he decided to give it another try. He returned for the 2000–01 season, played in 61 games, scored his first junior career goal and accumulated 245 penalty minutes. That year, he was also eligible for the NHL draft, and even though Boogaard did not have high expectations, he was overjoyed when the Minnesota Wild drafted him in the seventh round, 202nd overall.

The path to the NHL is not easy for some players, and Boogaard had to show some patience before finally getting the call to play with the Wild. After spending two more seasons in the Western Hockey League, he was signed to a professional contract with the Wild and was placed with the Louisiana IceGators in 2002–03 for conditioning and development. The Wild wanted a pure enforcer, and if they were willing to put in the time with him, Boogaard was willing to work for his dream. On top of skating lessons and practice, Boogaard took boxing lessons on the side to improve his fighting skills. Because of his height, he was expected to dominate all opponents, but Boogaard occasionally lost fights.

After accumulating 240 penalty minutes in just 33 games with the IceGators, the Wild moved Boogaard over to the Houston Aeros of the American Hockey League (AHL). After the 2003–04 season, Boogaard expected to be called up to play but was let down when the NHL lockout dashed his dreams of an NHL start. It was during that lockout season that Boogaard really came into his own as a fighter, winning the majority of his bouts with the other heavyweights of the AHL and garnering a legion of fans who cheered him on every time he stepped onto the ice.

He finally got his long-awaited wish and opened the 2005–06 season with the Wild. Within the first two weeks of the season, Boogaard had his first NHL goal, his first assist and his first fight, knocking the Anaheim Ducks Kip Brennan to the ice with a hard right. The rest of the season went well for Boogaard; he scored two goals, had four assists and chalked up 158 minutes in penalties. He did not get in many fights that season because his large frame and menacing looks were enough to keep most teams' tough guys at bay. But when he did fight, Boogaard's size and reach gave him a distinct advantage.

For the 2006–07 season, Boogaard appeared in only 48 games with the Wild but still led the club with 120 penalty minutes. His most infamous fight that season came in a game against the Anaheim Ducks. Squaring off against Todd Fedoruk, Boogaard beat the Ducks enforcer with three hard rights to the face that knocked Fedoruk to the ground and broke his jaw so severely that he had to have it surgically rebuilt with metal plates and wire meshing.

By the 2007–08 season, Boogaard had become one of the most popular players on the team and with fans. The fans appreciated his fierce style on the ice and his calmness and gentleness off the ice. Boogaard, though, was battling his own demons behind the scenes; he was taking prescription drugs to combat the pain from surgeries and to alleviate chronic back discomfort. His brother, Aaron, who also played in the NHL, said that Derek had to take extra pills for the medication to have any effect on him. "He'd go through 30 pills (Percocet) in a couple of days. He'd need 8 to 10 at a time to feel okay."

After undergoing surgery and missing out on games because of injury, Boogaard soon came to rely on his pain meds just to get through the day, and it wasn't long before he began to abuse the pills. He began spending thousands of dollars on OxyContin, hydrocodone and Vicodin, all in an effort to numb his pain. His addiction got so bad that Boogaard started missing practices, Wild management told other players not to give him any of their prescription medications, and he missed the training camp before the 2009–10 season. The team told the media that Boogaard was recovering from a concussion, but he was actually in a drug rehab center in southern California.

When Boogaard was released from the center, he returned to the Wild, but he fell back into his old ways. His teammates began to notice a change in him. "His demeanor, his personality, it just left him. He didn't have a personality anymore.

He just was kind of—a blank face," recalled teammate and friend John Scott.

Despite his off-ice problems, Boogaard finished out the rest of the 2009–10 season, playing in 57 games and accumulating 105 minutes in penalties. In the off-season, he became an unrestricted free agent. The Minnesota Wild offered him a contract that would effectively double his rookie salary, but for an enforcer of Boogaard's caliber, many other NHL teams were willing to pay larger amounts. The New York Rangers gave him the best offer, and he signed a four-year, $6.5-million contract. The deal was one of the higher priced contracts in the league for an enforcer, but the Rangers knew they were getting one of the best in the league.

"It's one of the great cities to be at and you're always on center stage when you're out there, so I'm excited," Boogaard told *The Star Tribune* of Minneapolis the night he signed.

The Rangers knew the risks behind signing Boogaard because of his past drug use, but all their fears were quickly put to rest when he started out the season by scoring just his third NHL goal and winning all of his fights. Rangers fans loved Boogaard, and if any opponents got out of hand at home games, the fans would begin to chant his name. The honeymoon didn't last long, however, as the constant physical toll on his body began to wear him down. After his second concussion, he was placed on injured reserve and told to wait until he recovered.

Watching the games on television and not being able to play was extremely difficult for Boogaard. He once again relapsed and began abusing prescription drugs and alcohol, often spending thousands of dollars at a time.

Concerned for the welfare of his son, Len Boogaard traveled to New York and was shocked by what he saw. Several times over the next several days, Len recalled his son crying in his arms.

"I had to hold him," said Len Boogaard. "It was like when he was younger, when he was a little kid growing up. He just sobbed away uncontrollably."

For months, Boogaard stayed in his $7000-per-month apartment, shutting out the world and everyone who wanted to get close to him. Friends began to notice that his memory was getting hazy, and he had lost the sunny, cheerful disposition he used to have.

In March 2011, Boogaard tried to resume light workouts with the Rangers, but the concussion symptoms were still present, and Rangers doctors continued to supply him with pills for his pain. Boogaard continued his descent into the world of drugs, and when he arrived at Madison

Square Garden clearly not focused and with his legs barely able to hold up his weight, the team sent him to rehab in California.

A few weeks later, after leaving rehab, Boogaard was back to his old habits. Then on the night of May 12, 2011, Boogaard mixed a dangerous combination of prescription pills and alcohol. The next morning, his brother Aaron found him dead in his bedroom. He was just 28 years old.

After his autopsy, it was discovered that Boogaard had been suffering from the same degenerative brain disease (chronic traumatic encephalopathy) that had afflicted Bob Probert. Some of the symptoms of the disease are that the person often suffers from depression, is prone to substance abuse and has memory problems.

Boogaard played in just 277 games, scoring three goals, getting 13 assists and recording 589 minutes in penalties.

Georges Laraque: Nice Tough Guy

I don't even like talking about fighting. It's an honor. As a kid, I was always the top scorer on my team. Would I rather have a good fight or a goal? I celebrate every goal like it's my last.

–Enforcer Georges Laraque

The first thing you notice about Georges Laraque when meeting him is that he is one of the nicest, most positive people in hockey despite being one of the toughest and strongest fighters to have skated in the NHL.

When Laraque first started playing hockey in his hometown of Montreal, he was one of the top goal scorers and wanted to be a superstar in the NHL like Mario Lemieux. Growing up wasn't easy for the son of Haitian immigrants. Playing in a predominantly white-dominated sport, Laraque was often singled out by opponents and even by fans watching the games, who felt they had the right to call him racist names. Laraque was bigger than most of the kids he played with and against, and when he was forced into a confrontation, he quickly resolved it. The racial abuse he received got so bad that his father removed him from hockey at the age of 12. But the lure of the sport was too strong, and Georges persuaded his parents to let him play again.

Laraque's size (he presently stands 6-foot-4 and weighs 245 pounds) gave him a competitive edge in front of the net and in the corners, making him one of the top scorers on his team. But as the other boys grew and caught up to Laraque, it quickly became apparent to him that he was no longer the best player on the ice and that if he wanted to make it into the NHL, he would have to find a different role.

Laraque entered the Quebec Major Junior Hockey League (QMJHL) in 1993 with the Saint-Jean Lynx. Although he began to play a more physical role, he could still put a few goals into the net, scoring 11 goals and getting 11 assists, along with 142 penalty minutes in 70 games in his rookie year. He followed that up with 19 goals, 22 assists and 259 penalty minutes in 62 games during the 1994–95 season with the Lynx.

After a solid season with the Lynx, Laraque finally got the moment he had been waiting for his whole life when, during the 1995 NHL Entry Draft, he was selected 31st overall by the Edmonton Oilers. The Oilers had some concerns about Laraque's skating ability, but the toughness and grit he could provide was something they needed at the time. He spent a few more year in the QMJHL, winning the Memorial Cup in 1996 with the Granby Predateurs, and then was moved to the Hamilton Bulldogs of the American Hockey League for further conditioning. Although he considered himself a power forward in the minors, when he finally got the call up to the NHL in 1997, he knew his role would be primarily as a fighter.

Within a few short seasons with the Oilers, Laraque had established himself as one of the toughest in the league. His size and sheer strength meant that not many other enforcers stepped up to the plate when he confronted them, so his penalty minutes per season do not really reflect the numbers of a top enforcer. When he wasn't required to drop the gloves, Laraque was more than happy to play hockey. He had his best scoring season in 2000–01, with 13 goals and 16 assists for 29 points. He also had the best game of his career that season when on February 21, 2000, he scored the only hat trick of his career and also got into a fight that night for good measure.

During his career, he went up against some of the toughest fighters of the time—Derek Boogaard, Darren McCarty, Brad May and Zdeno Chara—and held his own each time, more often than not coming out the victor. His style was fast and aggressive, always looking to grab the other guy quickly and get in as many right-handed punches before the referees stepped in.

After the 2004–05 lockout season, Laraque signed as a free agent with the Phoenix Coyotes with a one-year contract. At the end of that contract, Laraque played two seasons with the Pittsburgh Penguins and then two seasons in his hometown of Montreal, playing for the Canadiens before chronic back pain and other health issues forced him into retirement.

In the history of the NHL, not many enforcers would have been able to stand up to Laraque. He ended his career having played 695 games, scored 53 goals, had 100 assists and 1126 penalty minutes.

Ron Hextall: Mad Goalie

Ron Hextall was a goaltender unafraid of getting mixed up in a little physical action on the ice. While some goaltenders tend to shy away from on-ice brawls or scuffles, Hextall relished getting involved, which is one reason why he holds the dubious distinction as the most penalized goaltenders in NHL history.

Ron Hextall was born into hockey family royalty. His grandfather was Hall of Fame inductee Bryan Hextall, and his father Bryan Jr. and uncle Dennis Hextall all played more than 10 years in the NHL. As a young kid growing up in the '70s, he watched his father and uncle get roughed up by the Philadelphia Flyers, and he admitted hating the team that would eventually draft him.

Unlike his grandfather, father and uncle who all played forward positions, Ron Hextall chose to be a goaltender, but given his aggressive nature, he could easily have been a tough defenseman or perhaps an enforcer.

His fiery personality in goal caused many teams scouting the young Hextall to pass him over, but Philadelphia Flyers scout Gerry Melnyk thought the kid's temperament would fit well in a Flyers jersey. At the 1982 NHL Entry Draft, the Flyers selected the tall lanky goaltender 119th overall.

Playing for the Brandon Wheat Kings of the Western Hockey League, Hextall further solidified his reputation as a wild and unpredictable goaltender by accumulating 117 minutes in penalties during the 1983–84 season, a WHL record.

Hextall added to his reputation while playing for the Flyers American Hockey League farm team, the Hershey Bears. In the Calder Cup conference finals against the St. Catharines Saints, Hextall fought three different players in a bench-clearing brawl. This was the kind of player that suited the Flyers and head coach Mike Keenan, who finally decided to give the rookie a shot, allowing him to open the 1986–87 season.

Hextall won his first game playing with the Flyers and many more that season, but just because he was in the NHL did not mean he had changed his attitude. Hextall quickly established himself as a goalie who would not take lightly any sort of interference in front of his net. His weapon of choice was his stick, which he wielded like a lumberjack, hacking away at the opposing players' ankles and calves with impunity.

He also got into the odd fight, and in his first year, he took on the role of enforcer during a game against the New Jersey Devils. Early in the game, the Devils Steve Richmond punched Kjell Samuelson in the face, so Hextall skated down to the other end of the ice seeking out the

Devils goaltender Alain Chevrier in revenge. After pummeling the goaltender into the ice, Hextall only received a $300 fine for his actions.

In his rookie season, Hextall won 37 games and took home the Vezina Trophy as the league's most outstanding goaltender and culminated his rookie year with a trip to the Stanley Cup finals against the Edmonton Oilers. Hextall truly became one of the most notorious goaltenders when he started out game four with a 10-minute misconduct penalty for voicing his vehement displeasure over the Oilers fourth goal to the referee. He then received a five-minute major for slashing Kent Nilsson on the back of his knees. The incident was prompted by Oilers Glenn Anderson slashing Hextall as he was passing by the goaltender. Hextall didn't see who had originally slashed him, but after the game he showed no regrets for his actions.

"If somebody slaps you in the face, you're going to slap him back, it's not like he gave me a touch to jar the puck. What's he going to do next, break my arm? I'm sorry it was Nilsson and not Anderson I hit, but I just reacted. At the time, it seemed the right thing to do," said an unrepentant Hextall to reporters. He was suspended for eight games at the start of the following season.

Despite Hextall's performance, he managed to take the Stanley Cup final all the way to the seventh game, but unfortunately, the Flyers lost. However, Hextall was awarded the Conn Smythe Trophy for his heroics in the game, becoming only the fourth player from the losing team to win the award.

In each of Hextall's first two seasons in the NHL, he accumulated 104 minutes in penalties during the regular season, the first time in the history of the league a goaltender had over 100 penalty minutes. For the 1988–89 season, he bested his own record by accumulating 113 penalty minutes, and in the playoffs he found himself again at the center of an incident that earned him another suspension.

During game one of the Conference finals against the Montreal Canadiens, the Flyers Brian Propp was knocked unconscious by an elbow from Canadiens defenseman Chris Chelios. Hextall felt that Chelios had never paid the price for his actions, so in game six with the Canadiens just a few minutes from winning the game, being up 4–2 in the third and the series, Hextall left his crease when Chelios skated into the Flyers zone, and he attacked the Canadiens defenseman, punching him several times with the blunt end of his blocker. Naturally, a scuffle ensued, and as the referee was escorting the goaltender off the ice, Hextall kept challenging Canadiens goaltender Patrick Roy to take off his helmet and fight him.

After a few more seasons with the Flyers, Hextall was traded to the Quebec Nordiques in the mega Lindros deal. Hextall spent only one season with the Nordiques and another with the Islanders before making it back to the Flyers, where he ended his career in 1999, never having won the Stanley Cup but making his mark nonetheless.

Honorable Mention: Zdeno Chara

There have been few true NHL enforcers able to stand up to the big Slovak defenseman, and at 6-foot-8, Zdeno Chara, "The Giant," has stood up against the best of them over his long career.

Although not classified as a fighter, Chara joined the NHL in 1997 after being drafted by the New York Islanders, where he quickly earned a reputation as a strong, physically intimidating player. He didn't drop the gloves much when playing for the Islanders, but after being traded to the Ottawa Senators in 2001, he began taking on a more physical role. Most of his fights followed a similar pattern: a player would get upset with Chara or he would challenge them, gloves would hit the ice then Chara would completely manhandle his opponent, tossing him around like a rag doll.

Although he did fight against much bigger opponents such as Georges Laraque and Ratis Ivannas, the fights never lasted long. Experienced fighters like Laraque were able to match Chara in strength, get him off balance and put him down. However, apart from one or two players currently in the NHL, Chara is pretty much a force unto himself, and he is often accused of bullying the other players and using his size to intimidate them.

One of the most famous incidents happened on March 8, 2011, in a game between the Montreal Canadiens and Chara's Boston Bruins (Chara was traded to the team in 2006). Before that game there had been a few run-ins between Canadiens forward Max Pacioretty and Chara, including one in which Pacioretty taunted Chara after scoring a goal.

The March 8 incident between the two players was much worse and nearly cost Pacioretty his life. During the game, Pacioretty and Chara were both skating hard toward the Bruins zone along the boards, chasing a loose puck. Pacioretty was on the inside trying to pass by Chara when the Boston captain used his massive frame to push Pacioretty's head into the stanchion (the padded edge of the glass surrounding the ice) at the end of the Canadiens bench.

The entire Bell Centre went silent the instant Pacioretty's lifeless body hit the ice. For a few minutes, the Canadiens forward did not move at all. Fortunately, he regained consciousness and was removed from the ice on a stretcher.

Chara meanwhile received a major penalty and was ejected from the game.

The next day, doctors revealed that Pacioretty had suffered a severe concussion and a fracture to his vertebra. Montreal Canadiens fans were sure Chara would receive a suspension for the hit as it clearly showed in the replay that Chara guided Pacioretty's head into the thinly padded stanchion. Chara was not penalized. The NHL vice president of hockey operations, the man responsible for handing out suspensions, deemed the incident a "hockey play" and an unfortunate accident. Montreal police announced a criminal investigation into the hit but later dropped the case.

Despite his reputation as a physical player, Chara is also a Norris Trophy–winning defenseman, and he won the Stanley Cup in 2011 as the captain of the Boston Bruins.

~ Chapter 5 ~

There Is No "I" in Team

The people who yell and scream about hockey violence are a handful of intellectuals and newspapermen who never pay to get in to see a game. The fans, who shell out the money, have always liked good, rough hockey.

–Don Cherry

The Broad Street Bullies

We take the shortest route to the puck and arrive in ill humor.

–Bobby Clarke, captain of the Philadelphia Flyers

When the Philadelphia Flyers joined the NHL after the 1967 expansion, they were a team of aging veterans and career minor leaguers. They managed to cobble together a decent team over the next few years, but they had limited success against the established Original Six clubs such as Montreal, Boston and Chicago. The original six teams were rife with talent and had established farm systems that kept the teams replenished for years, making it difficult for the expansion teams such as the Flyers to compete for a Stanley Cup championship. If they were going to beat teams like the Canadiens and the Bruins, the Flyers could not rely on talent alone. The man to realize that the Flyers needed a new direction was Keith Allen.

After coaching the Flyers from 1967 to 1969, Keith Allen became well aware of what was missing on the team. Allen and general manager Bud Poile had tried to build a fast, skilled team that could play the brand of hockey played in the Original Six era. During the regular season, the Flyers slowly began to show that they could compete, winning tough games against Boston and Montreal. However, in the playoffs, the Flyers learned a hard lesson. In their first two appearances in the playoffs, they were matched up against their division rivals, the St. Louis Blues, and Philadelphia was bludgeoned into submission.

The Blues Noel Picard and the Plager brothers, Barclay and Bob, terrorized the Flyers, with most of the games ending up in all-out brawls. The Flyers Claude LaForge got the worst of the Blues' brand of rough hockey when he was sucker punched by Noel Picard in the middle of a brawl.

LaForge ended up unconscious with five teeth missing and a fractured cheekbone and eye socket. After those two playoff series against the Blues, Flyers management decided to toughen up their lineup. The Flyers fired Bud Poile and appointed Keith Allen as the new general manager to oversee the team's change in philosophy, which began with the 1969 NHL Amateur Draft.

At the draft, the Flyers' selections spoke to their new direction when they took Dave Schultz and Don Saleski in the fifth and sixth rounds. However, the fate of the franchise was sealed earlier in the draft when the Flyers selected a young player nobody wanted because of his history of diabetes. Bobby Clarke was passed over several times before the Flyers took a chance with him. Clarke ended up as the face of the franchise and the captain of the two-time Stanley Cup champions.

Despite Clarke's successful rookie season, the Flyers regressed in the standings, missed out on the playoffs in 1970 and were taken out in the first round in 1971. The team needed an identity, so for the 1971–72 season, two key changes were made. Head coach Vic Stasiuk was fired and replaced by Fred Shero, and Dave Schultz was brought up from the farm team. Those two additions changed the future of the club.

Suddenly, with the addition of Schultz, the Flyers had someone who could stand up to all those players who had beaten the team in the past. In his first game with the Flyers, Schultz got into a fight, and then in his second game, another fight. The message he sent to the rest of the league was clear: mess with my team and you're gonna have to pay for it. The message also spread to the rest of the Flyers, who soon they got involved in those battles and pasted the ice with blood. The team's new philosophy of "toughness first and skill second" was promoted by head coach Fred Shero and executed by a team of bullies.

Shero, the strange and mysterious former boxer and lover of philosophy, was the perfect coach for the Broad Street Bullies. "I had a team that loved to fight, so I let them fight," he once said. Shero was unlike his team in so many ways, but that's what they needed behind the bench. An introverted student of the game, Shero was a quiet, cerebral coach who never really spoke to his players but got the best out of them when he needed to.

When he did communicate with his players outside game time, he often left notes in the players' lockers or inspirational and sometimes strange quotations on the blackboard, such as, "The person who 'has it made' is only one step from being a has-been." "There are no heroic tales, without heroic tails." "I have a reason for living. Satisfaction is death." "To avoid criticism, say nothing, do nothing, BE nothing." "People usually get what's coming to them—unless it has been mailed."

The Flyers players knew Shero was a little bit of an odd ball, but they knew he had a winning formula.

There had never been a team like the Flyers in the NHL before—winning hockey games through sheer intimidation. For the Flyers, fighting was as legitimate a tactic as any other, and it worked. By the 1972–73 season, the Flyers achieved their desired goal of forming an identity, and they even had a name to go with it.

On January 4, 1973, Jack Chevalier of the *Philadelphia Daily News* wrote an article about the Flyers' style of hockey, with the headline, "Broad Street Bullies Muscle Atlanta," referring to a particularly violent game with the Atlanta Flames the night before. The name stuck.

For the 1972–73 season, the Broad Street Bullies tallied an incredible 600 penalty minutes more than the second most penalized team, the St. Louis Blues. The fists of Dave "The Hammer" Schultz, Bob "Hound" Kelly, Don "Big Bird" Saleski and Andre "Moose" Dupont combined for over 800 penalty minutes that season; incredibly, it was more than the totals for six of the NHL clubs.

For the playoffs that season, the Broad Street Bullies pounded their way to their first franchise series' win, beating the Minnesota North Stars four games to two. The Flyers, though, lost in the second round to the much more refined Montreal Canadiens and the goaltending of Ken Dryden.

After that loss, the Flyers added the final pieces of their team to make them a true Stanley Cup competitor. In the offseason, GM Keith Allen acquired Bernie Parent, the eccentric French Canadian goaltender who infused the team with a whole new level of confidence. With Parent in nets, Bobby Clarke, Bill Barber, Rick MacLeish and Reggie Leach scoring the goals, and Schultz and Kelly policing the ice, the Flyers battled their way to the top tier of the league and became one of the most difficult teams to play against.

Before long, the team that could barely get in a few thousand fans to watch their games when they first entered the league was now selling out seats every night. Philadelphia fans became as loud and as raucous as their team; they were a blue-collar city with a blue-collar team. The city had been starving for a winning team for years when along came these crazy Canadian players that united the city.

The 1973–74 Flyers captured the West Division with 112 points, winning 50 games and losing just 16. They also finished the season with 1750 penalty minutes, again completely eclipsing the rest of the league in that category. In the playoffs, the Flyers beat their way past the Atlanta Flames in four straight games in a series that was filled with fights, bloodied faces and bench-clearing brawls.

In the semifinals, the Flyers had to walk into Madison Square Garden to try to beat the New York Rangers. In the history of the franchise, the Flyers had won only one game in Madison Square Garden. Despite the fact that no expansion franchise had ever beat an Original Six team in the playoffs, the Flyers managed to win in a fight- and blood-filled seven-game series. The Broad Street Bullies muscled their way into the Stanley Cup final against Bobby Orr and the Boston Bruins.

The Bruins were the heavy favorites to win the series, but the Flyers surprised everyone and won the franchise's first Stanley Cup. They won their second Stanley Cup, beating the Buffalo Sabres in the 1975 playoffs.

The Broad Street Bullies had triumphed and forever changed the face of hockey. Hockey purists hated to watch the Flyers' brand of hockey, which bordered on criminal behavior. The Flyers became the evil empire, and many NHL executives were beginning to question the direction the team was taking the game. But as much as the league discussed the disgraceful behavior of the Flyers on the ice, none of their players was ever penalized or suspended unless warranted. Violence sells, and the Flyers were bringing new legions of fans to the game.

The era of the Broad Street Bullies could not last forever, however, and the first sign of their fall came in a pre-season game before the start of the 1975–76 season against the Montreal Canadiens. The Canadiens quickly figured out that the best way to beat the Flyers was to play like the Flyers, and rather than be intimidated, the Canadiens started an all-out brawl.

That season, the Canadiens finished on top of the league with 127 points followed by the Flyers with 118 points, and as fate would have it, the two teams met in the Stanley Cup finals. The entire hockey world was pulling for the Canadiens that year because they wanted to show that skill and class won Stanley Cups, not physical violence. The Canadiens played with skill and grace but also added some violence of their own that series, led by big defenseman Larry Robinson. The Canadiens were on a mission to retake the Holy Grail from the heathens and ready to match the Flyers in every way. "If you're going to school and this big bully keeps coming up and bothering you, how do you counteract that?

You fight fire with fire. So we stood up to them," said Robinson. The Canadiens put the Broad Street Bullies out to pasture, but for two glorious seasons, the Flyers were at the top of the food chain, and no one dared to challenge them.

The Broad Street Bullies did something more than just win two Stanley Cups—they changed the way hockey could be played. It was now a game where intimidation became as useful a tool as another team's top scoring line or hot goaltender. The idea of using intimidation as a tactic quickly spread throughout the league, and while no other team came close to the tactics of the Broad Street Bullies, franchises made it a goal in future drafts to bring into the NHL guys like Dave Schultz, who could pound the opposition with impunity and hopefully give their team an advantage. Within a few seasons, every team near the bottom of the league employed one or two enforcers, ushering in a new style of hockey that exists, in part, even to this day.

The Shoe Brawl

The game on December 23, 1979, was regularly contentious between the Boston Bruins and the New York Rangers at Madison Square Garden. In the final seconds of the third period, with the Bruins leading the game 4–3, Rangers forward (and former Bruin) Phil Esposito broke into the Bruins zone on a breakaway but was stopped by goaltender Gerry Cheevers. A few seconds later, the whistle sounded, and Esposito smashed his stick on the ice in anger. All seemed well and calm while the Bruins congratulated each other at center ice and prepared to go to their dressing room. The Rangers players, a little unhappy at the outcome of the game, wanted to say a few words to the Bruins, and a scuffle ensued.

While all the players from both teams were pressed up against the boards, pushing and shoving, a few fans thought they would help the Rangers take on the Bruins. One fan, maybe after a few too many beers, used that evening's game program to smack Bruins tough guy Stan Jonathan in the face. Madison Square Garden at the time had low glass along the side boards, giving fans unsafe access to the players. The unwise attack drew Jonathan's blood, and the fan compounded the insult by stealing Jonathan's stick and swinging it around like an axe, trying to hit his teammates. Bruins enforcer Terry O'Reilly witnessed the assault and decided to take the fight into the stands. He leapt over the glass, grabbed the fan and began to pound away just like he would any opposing player on the ice. The fan had entered his world, and O'Reilly was not going to treat him any differently than he would another player.

It did not take long before other members of the Bruins scaled the glass and joined in the melee. One fan in particular caught the eye of Bruins forward Peter McNab. As the fan tried to scurry for the exit, McNab grabbed him by the shoulders and tossed him to the ground. Fellow teammate Mike Milbury soon joined McNab and grabbed the fan's legs, then removed his shoe and proceeded to repeatedly strike him with it. In total, 18 Bruins went into the stands, even Bruins general manager Harry Sinden got involved, trying to separate his players from the crowd before a fan got seriously hurt.

Eventually, calm was restored, the police arrested the fans, and the teams returned to their dressing rooms. For jumping into the stands, Terry O'Reilly was suspended for eight games, and Peter McNab and Mike Milbury both received six-game suspensions. The only Bruin not on the ice for the game was winning goaltender Gerry Cheevers, who said jokingly that by the time the other guys got back to the dressing room, "I was already on my second beer."

After the game, Phi Esposito blamed the low glass in Madison Square Garden as the cause of the fight after the game. "You go to other towns like Pittsburgh, they have the small glass and guys are spitting at you and they're throwing whiskey or beer in your face.... You get angry because you're in the game for an hour or something and you've been banged all over the ice and you've been taking abuse and yelling and screaming from 15,000 people and you lose your temper," he said.

Looking back on the moment, Milbury laughed it off. "Worst thing I did, I think, that night was I took the shoe and threw it on the ice, so he was going home that night with one shoe on and one shoe off," he said. "Of all the things throughout my career, you know, 13 years in professional hockey, no matter what I've done or will do in the future, I will live with the shoe."

The Battle of Quebec

Rivalry between teams is what makes hockey exciting for fans. What would hockey be without the rivalry between Montreal and Toronto, Calgary against Edmonton or the Flyers and the Penguins? For the fans, it's a great way to bond with their home team and ignite a passion for the game. That passion, though, is not exclusive to the fans; it sometimes it spills down onto the ice.

One of the greatest and bloodiest rivalries in hockey history was between the Quebec Nordiques and the Montreal Canadiens in the 1980s and early '90s. However, it is impossible to understand the bad blood between the two clubs without a subtle appreciation of the social and political context of the time. Quebec was in an internal battle over the future of its place in Canada. The Parti Quebecois had almost led the province and its people to separation, but during the 1980 referendum, they were narrowly defeated by Quebecers who wanted to stay within Canada. As often happens in Quebec, politics, society and sports get mixed together, and the Canadiens and Nordiques were thrown into this cauldron.

The Canadiens were the storied franchise of the NHL, representing in Quebeckers' minds the establishment, while the Nordiques, wearing the light blue and fleur-de-lis jerseys, were the embodiment of the separatist movement rolling through the province. It was a phenomenon that was dividing families all across Quebec.

Montreal Canadiens forward Guy Carbonneau said at the time that players' families fought because of the rivalry and argued about which team deserved to reign over the hearts and minds of the people of the province. All that emotion was played out on the ice between two teams battling for a place in the Stanley Cup finals.

The battle of Quebec began during the 1979– 80 season when the Quebec Nordiques joined the NHL. Although initially the rivalry was not that intense because the Nordiques spent the first two seasons in a different division, passions began to rise in 1982. That's when the Canadiens moved into the Nordiques division, and for the first time the two teams met in the playoffs.

The series was ground zero for their mutual hatred of each other. After losing the opening game, the Nordiques won the next two games, putting them in a good spot to clinch the best-of-five series. But the Canadiens came storming back in the fourth game, winning 6–2. It was in this fourth game that things got a little out of hand. The referee handed out 251 minutes in penalties, 159 minutes in the first period alone.

In the fifth and deciding game, the two teams battled hard, but it was the Nordiques that came out on top when Dale Hunter scored 22 seconds into the overtime period to send the Canadiens packing.

The rivalry reached epic proportions in 1984 when the two teams met in the playoffs for a second time and played a game that would come to be known as the "Good Friday Massacre." By game six of the seven-game series, Montreal had taken a 3–2 series lead, and the team was hoping to move on with a win before a hometown crowd. Game six was held in Montreal on April 20, 1984, and the Canadiens got their wish, winning the game by a score of 5–3 and moving on into the next round.

However, that sixth game is best remembered for the multiple brawls that started as the second period was coming to a close. Nordiques Dale Hunter pinned Canadiens forward Guy Carbonneau to the ice, starting a bench-clearing brawl where even the goalies got involved. Referees could do little as players paired up and began trading punches. Order was eventually restored, and the players were sent to their dressing rooms while referees sorted out the penalties.

When the teams returned to the ice for the start of the third period, before the puck was dropped, another brawl broke out in an attempt to settle accounts from the previous period's punching match. Players piled on top of players, sucker punches were thrown and players hunted each other looking for revenge. The referees threw 10 players out of the game and handed out over 250 minutes in penalties. The brawl most likely favored the Canadiens since they were still down in the game at the start of the third period, and after things quieted down and the game continued, they finished off the game with a 5–3 win.

After the brawl, debates began to rage in the news and on the radio about hockey's state of affairs.

"Shame on you, Montreal Canadiens. You were a disgrace to the uniform," wrote *Montreal*

Gazette columnist Michael Farber. "Shame on you, Quebec Nordiques. After spending the last two years trying to polish your image, you helped turn a playoff game into what would be mere burlesque if the fights weren't premeditated."

Most people were disgusted by the outcome of the game. Even the head coach of the Nordiques, Michel Bergeron, was disappointed by the level of violence in the game. "Too bad there were children all over the province watching this. Too bad," he said.

The public supported making changes in the NHL to rule out all violent incidents like the game in Montreal, but the NHL only paid lip service to the problem. League officials failed to grasp the opportunity, and so the debate continues to rage to this day.

The teams met again in the 1985 playoffs, but the players were remarkably civil in comparison to the playoffs the year earlier. The Nordiques won that series in game seven on a goal by Peter Stastny. The Canadiens won the next time the teams met in the 1987 playoffs and again in 1993, the year they won the Cup. The rivalry died in 1995 when the Quebec Nordiques folded operations and moved to Denver to become the Colorado Avalanche.

The Punch-up in Piestany

Before 1987, international hockey tournaments between nations had been largely peaceful affairs. The teams played hard but fair hockey most of the time, respecting the international rules of the sport that disallowed fighting. The international game was a place to see hockey at its best, not a place for physical violence, but all that changed after the Canadian junior team played the Soviet juniors in Piestany, Czechoslovakia, on January 4, 1987. The game re-ignited a national debate about the state of affairs of North American hockey and was the impetus for a growing belief across the continent that fighting should have no place in the game.

Canada and the Soviet Union had been engaged in an increasingly bitter and intense hockey rivalry since the communists first appeared and won the 1954 World Ice Hockey Championship, defeating the Canadians in the gold medal game by a score of 7–2. From 1963 to 1983, the Soviets won 17 World Championship titles, completely dominating international hockey. The rules stated that these tournaments were supposed to be played by amateurs, but the Canadians and other countries long suspected the Russians were sending in professionals. The controversy led to more tensions between the two countries, with Canada's eventual boycotting of the World

Championships and the Olympic hockey tournaments from 1970 to 1976.

The lack of success on the international stage left many Canadians questioning whether hockey was still their game. The answer came during the 1972 Summit Series. Canada's best played against the Soviets' best to decide once and for all which nation could claim the rights to hockey supremacy. Canada won that battle, thanks to the winning goal by Paul Henderson, but the cold war continued between the two nations and the fierce rivalry only intensified.

In 1977, Canada's junior players got involved in the global hockey war with the creation of the World Junior Championship. The Soviets had won five gold medals since 1982, and the Canadians none. Up until that time, Hockey Canada had sent the Memorial Cup champions to defend Canadian hockey, but 1982 was the first time a national junior team composed of the best junior players in Canada would play, and they won. The Soviets won two gold medals after that, and Canada won in 1985. The war between the two teams heating up again. After winning another gold in 1986, the Soviets were looking to put the Canadians away with a decisive victory at the 1987 World Juniors in Piestany.

The Canadian national team at the 1987 Canada Cup sent a definitive message to the Soviet

national team when they won as a result of Mario
Lemieux's dramatic goal from a pass by Wayne
Gretzky. Canada had reasserted itself as a dominant hockey force, and at the 1987 World Juniors,
the young players were looking to put the icing
on the cake with a gold medal win.

The 1987 World Junior Championship in Piestany was organized in a round-robin format,
meaning that the teams with the top three
records after playing a total of seven games were
given the gold, silver and bronze, respectively
(ties were decided via goal differential). Finland
finished their schedule with a 5–1–1 record to
lead the tournament. Canada entered their last
game of the tournament with a record of 4–1–1
and had already been assured a bronze medal.
Canada's final opponents, the Russians, entered
the game with a 2–3–1 record, which meant they
were out of medal contention.

To win the gold medal, all Canada had to do
was score four goals on the Soviets to pass Finland in the goal differential. The final game
between the Soviets and the Canadian was purposely scheduled because organizers believed
that one of the teams would be in the final hunt
for gold, and they wanted another country to
have a shot at a gold medal.

Before the game even started, tensions were
mounting. Team Canada's main worry was the

appointment of inexperienced Norwegian referee Hans Ronning. The concerns about Ronning came about during an earlier game between Canada and the United States and his handling of a pre-game brawl. Ronning had not been on the ice at the time of the fight but decided to eject one player from each team at random for starting the brawl. The two players were barred from the game that night and also for the next game— whether they were actually took part in the brawl was of little consequence to Ronning.

For such an important game against the Soviets, Canada did not want to take any risks, so they petitioned the International Ice Hockey Federation to find a more experienced referee. They were turned down flat. Already the game was looking to have the potential for fireworks, and the puck had not yet been dropped.

On game day, January 4, 1987, Canada's lineup included such future NHL standouts as Theoren Fleury, Glen Wesley, Steve Chiasson, Mike Keane, Brendan Shanahan and Pierre Turgeon. The Soviets had a equally skilled lineup with Vladimir Konstantinov, Sergei Fedorov, Valeri Zelepukin, Vladimir Malakhov and Alexander Mogilny.

Team Canada's worries came to fruition at the opening faceoff when Sergei Shesterikov elbowed Canada's Dave McLlwain, who then responded with a cross-check. Ronning did not assess either player a penalty. With the referee not setting the tone of the game or taking control early on, the tension began to escalate further.

Five minutes into the game, Theoren Fleury opened the scoring for Canada. He celebrated the goal by sliding across the ice on his knees and acting as if he was shooting the Soviet bench with his hockey stick. His actions did not help foster warm feelings between the two teams.

As the period progressed, the Soviets and the Canadians hacked and slashed at each other, while the Norwegian referee continued to look the other way. By the end of the first period, Canada had taken a 3–1 lead, needing just one more goal to guarantee a gold medal victory.

During the first intermission, Theoren Fleury was interviewed by the CBC and referred to the intensity of the play. "The boys are up for the gold medal. Everybody is so tense. Tempers are flying. It's really tough out there…. I can't believe it. It's so tense. It's so tense."

Before the start of the second period, a moment of silence was observed in memory of four members of the Swift Current Broncos who were killed when their team bus crashed five days earlier. As a result, the opening five minutes of the second period were played with less intensity, but after one or two errant slashes and high elbows, all the good feelings vanished, and both teams were back to hacking away at each other. Things began to devolve even further when the Canadians scored their fourth goal, assuring them of the gold medal. The Soviets had nothing left to lose.

At about the six-minute mark in the second, Shesterikov collided with Canadian Everett Sanipass, touching off a fight between the two players; then Pavel Kostichkin gave Fleury a wicked two-handed slash, leading to another fight. The scene degenerated into a brawl among all the players on the ice.

Complete chaos erupted when Evgeny Davydov left the Soviet bench to join in the fight. Once he did that, the Canadian bench emptied, and a full-scale brawl broke out. Officials tried at first to break the teams apart, but their attempts were futile. The officials left the ice and let the mayhem reign.

Canada's Mike Keane paired off against Valeri Zelepukin and wailed blows down on him like a professional boxer, at one point even losing his jersey and shoulder pads. For the Soviets, Konstantinov leveled Greg Harwood with a headbutt that broke his nose. At one point during the brawl, almost every player from both benches was involved in some sort of punch-up or wrestling match.

Not knowing how to control the situation, the stadium officials shut off the lights in the hopes of calming things down, while the fans in attendance whistled and booed the players. But once the lights were turned back on, the fighting continued. The brawl lasted about five minutes until calm was restored. As fighting and especially brawls are not allowed at the World Juniors, the game was declared null and void by the International Ice Hockey Federation (IIHF).

Off ice, an emergency meeting between the participating countries was convened, and the delegates voted in favor of ejecting both teams from the tournament. They also decided that the Soviets would be banned from the medal ceremony and the tournament banquet following the game but that the Canadian team would be allowed to attend even though they had been stripped of their medal.

Team Canada delegate Dennis McDonald was so incensed at the decision to disqualify Canada for what he saw as the other member countries (Finland, Sweden, Czechoslovakia in particular) voting him down because they all stood to gain medals with Canada's expulsion. McDonald's dismissal of the IIHF decision was less than cordial, angering IIHF president Gunther Sabetzki who along with the Czechoslovakian officials, responded by kicking the Canadian team out of the arena. Armed guards escorted the team across the border and out of the country.

The aftermath continued in the media for months after the game. The entire Soviet team was suspended for six months from competing in international tournaments, and the coaches were given a three-year ban. Among the Canadians, only two players were not given the same punishment: goaltender Jimmy Waite and forward Pierre Turgeon.

Waite argued that he did not fight because he did not want to risk getting thrown out of the game if it was going to continue. Turgeon never really gave an answer as to why he did not engage in the fight, but some of his teammates were none too happy with him.

"I'm looking for someone to help (Stephane) Roy out and I look over at the bench. There's this dog Turgeon, just sitting there with his head down," said Canadian forward Everett Sanipass. "He wouldn't get his ass off the bench...just sitting there when everyone's off the Soviet bench, and at least one of our guys is in real trouble getting double-teamed."

The entire affair set off a great debate in Canada about the soul of the game. Phone lines at radio stations lit up with callers, some praising the Canadians for standing up for themselves while other callers were disappointed that the gold medal was taken away because of the brawl and how the incident reflected on Canadian hockey in general.

One of the most vocal supporters of the Canadian players was the self-appointed keeper of all things sacred in the good ole hockey game, Don Cherry. For him, the blame lay in one place and in one place only, and that was with the Soviets.

"I blame the Russians, naturally, anybody with any mind would blame the Russians," said Cherry in a CBC interview.

It seemed that the Soviets did start the brawl on purpose to force the Canadians into forfeiting their gold medal, but the other side of the argument said that the Canadians should not have even got involved in the fight given that the gold medal was on the line. If the Canadian players had simply skated away from the Soviets and sought refuge on the bench, they would have been awarded the gold medal.

For Cherry, the brawl was about pride and protecting your fellow teammates, but for others it was about being smart and avoiding trouble. Overwhelmingly, most Canadians agreed with Don Cherry. While they lamented the loss of the gold medal, standing up to the Soviet thug players was deemed by most to be the right and honorable thing to do.

Wanting to do something for the Canadian players, Toronto Maple Leafs owner Harold Ballard went so far as to have gold medals made for the players. "I believe the Canadian boys deserve the gold medal and I'm going to see to it that they get them," said Ballard. "Imagine how these Russians engineered this whole thing over there just because they've got a lousy team and were scared to go home in sixth place."

Whatever side of the debate people landed on, the brawl did accomplish one thing. Before the brawl in Piestany, coverage of the World Junior Tournament was spotty, and Canadians showed little interest in the series, but today, it is one of the most anticipated tournaments for hockey fans in Canada, second only to Winter Olympic hockey tournaments and maybe the World Hockey Championship.

The Brawl in Hockeytown

On May 29, 1996, the Detroit Red Wings and the Colorado Avalanche were involved in a heated battle for the privilege of moving on to play in the Stanley Cup final. It was game six of the Western Conference finals, and the Avalanche were trying to send the Red Wings packing. The series had been hard fought but fair for the most part until game six, with about five minutes left in the first period. Kris Draper, the Red Wings' hard-checking forward, was making a play along the boards and turned his back for a mere second when Avalanche forward Claude Lemieux checked him hard from behind, sending his face into the top edge of the boards. Draper's jaw and nose were broken and he suffered a concussion. Lemieux was given a five-minute penalty and ejected from the game.

The Avalanche won the game, and after the traditional handshake at the end of the series, Red Wings forward Dino Ciccarelli famously stated about Lemieux, "I can't believe I shook this guy's friggin' hand after the game. That pisses me right off."

As for NHL justice, the league gave Lemieux a two-game suspension, which to Detroit was an insult. Over the summer, the Red Wings had time to ponder the playoff loss, of the insulting injury to one of their most respected players and of watching Claude Lemieux raise the Cup over his head after the Avalanche defeated the Florida Panthers in the Stanley Cup finals.

The moment the series was over, sports pundits and fans were already checking their calendars waiting for the next time the two teams would meet the following season. The Red Wings had a score to settle with the Avalanche and especially with Lemieux.

Surprisingly, when the two teams met up for the first time in the 1996–97 season, nothing out of the ordinary occurred. They played each other two more times without incident that season, but on the night of March 26, 1997, the flood gates opened and all hell broke loose.

No incidents had occurred in the earlier games because Lemieux had not dressed for any of those match-ups. However, for the fourth game in Detroit against the Wings, Lemieux suited up and was thrown to the lions. Tensions were clearly high in the first period as Avalanche defenseman Brent Severyn and Wings defenseman Jamie Pushor started the night off with a fight two minutes into the first period. The bout was followed by another fight between Wings Kirk Matlby and Avs Rene Corbet at the 10-minute mark of the first.

With a few minutes left in the first period, Lemieux stepped out onto the ice, and the Red Wings seized their chance for revenge. During a scuffle after a mid-ice collision between the Avs Peter Forsberg and the Wings Igor Larionov, Red Wings tough guy Darren McCarty took advantage of the distracted officials trying to break up the melee and hit Lemieux on the side of his face. McCarty got in a few more punches before

Lemieux turtled on the ice. McCarty swung for any open spot, dragging him along the ice and yelling at him to stand up. McCarty managed to knee Lemieux in the ribs before the linesmen jumped in.

This perceived assault on Lemieux touched off several more fights until a full-out brawl ensued. While McCarty was raining fists down on Lemieux,

Avs goaltender Patrick Roy skated out to help his teammate, but Red Wings forward Brendan Shanahan intercepted him with an open-ice body check. The check sent both players flying through the air. Avs defenseman Adam Foote immediately came to his goaltender's defense and began a tussle with Shanahan. Meanwhile, Red Wings Mike Vernon saw Roy in the fight and raced out into the fray and got into a punch-up with Roy that ended in both goaltenders bleeding from cuts to their faces. Eventually, while officials got control of the game and handed out penalties, the Zamboni had to be called out to clean up the blood on the ice.

Officials hoped the brawl had settled accounts between the teams, but just 15 seconds after play resumed, the Avs Adam Deadmarsh and Wings Vladimir Konstantinov dropped their gloves. Before the end of the third period, five more fights occurred. Sometime in the midst of the chaos, a few goals were scored, and the Wings won the contest 6–5 in overtime on a Darren McCarty goal.

After the game, McCarty commented on the fighting. "Guys just paired off. I guess it was just God's will I got paired off with Lemieux," he said with a big smile across his face. "Forsberg started the whole thing. But that's the way hockey is. Sometimes things like that happen when you're seven years old, and you have to wait until you're 10 to get back at the guy. Some guys are still getting even for things that happened when they were kids. You just wait for your chances. It was intense."

Avs defenseman Adam Foote commented on Patrick Roy's performance. "You've got to have a lot of respect for Patrick, getting into it, a guy like that. He didn't have to do something like that," he said.

This was not the end, however, as the Red Wings still felt that Lemieux had not answered for what he had done. He had his chance to end it in his fight with McCarty, but they felt he had chosen the coward's way out and turtled until the linesmen rescued him. The bad blood continued into the playoffs in the Conference finals where the hockey gods ensured the two clubs would meet.

Another brawl broke out in the course of the series, and even the coaches got involved, with Avs head coach Marc Crawford climbing onto the glass separating the benches to scream at Wings head coach Scotty Bowman. Detriot got the most important revenge in that series, defeating the Avs and going on to win the Stanley Cup. But the win still was not good enough for the players and their original grudge with Lemieux. Despite all the hits to their heads, hockey players have good memories.

The Red Wings finally got their chance to air their gripes with Lemieux during a November game in the 1997–98 season. At the opening faceoff, Red Wings enforcer Darren McCarty lined up beside the Avs Claude Lemieux, and finally, Lemieux agreed to drop the gloves. The two traded punches, and the fight ended in a draw, presumably ending the bad blood.

However, when the two clubs later squared off on April 1, 1998, another melee broke out at center ice. Patrick Roy skated into the mix and challenged a reluctant Wings goaltender Chris Osgood to a fight. The officials tried to keep the two netminders apart, but Roy was determined to get at his target. Osgood and Roy began trading punches. Fans watching the game at home will remember the Colorado television play-by-play announcer screaming with delight as Roy pounded Osgood. With each punch, the announcer screamed, "Another right by Roy! Another right by Roy! Another right! Uppercut! Yeah! You better believe it, baby!"

The rivalry continued for another few years, but as players were traded to other teams or lost to retirement, the bad blood between the two clubs faded, their rivalry now resigned to the pages of history.

The Most Penalized Game in Hockey

The 2003–04 Ottawa Senators were not known as a violent team, neither really were the Philadelphia Flyers that season, but when the two teams met on March 5, 2004, the level of violence that occurred broke records.

The brawl had been ignited a week earlier likely because of an incident between the Flyers Marck Recchi and the Senators Martin Havlat. In the third period, as Recchi skated back to his zone to defend on an Ottawa rush, he was shadowing Havlat closely. Going at top speed into the corner to retrieve the puck, Recchi hooked Havlat, tripping him up and sending both players crashing into the boards. Havlat was none too happy about the hook. He brought his stick up and slashed at Recchi's head. Havlat was assessed a five-minute major and a game misconduct. After the game, Havlat was apologetic, "I don't feel good about what I did," he said. "I wanted to hit him but not in the face. It was a bad decision, and we'll see what happens."

The apology, however, was not enough for Flyers head coach Ken Hitchcock, who hinted that retribution could be coming down the line. "Some day, someone's going to make him eat his lunch," said Hitchcock. "This is something, in my opinion, that the players should take care of."

Recchi let his future intentions toward Havlat be known: "He's that type of player. He's done it before. It might not come from our team. But he better protect himself."

Havlat was suspended for his actions for two games. His first game back with the Senators was on March 5, 2004, against the Flyers.

On the night of the rematch, the Senators expected some sort of payback from the Flyers, but what happened surprised everyone. The game went through two periods without any real incidents and only a few minor penalties here and there. With just under two minutes left in the game, the Flyers were winning 5–2 and playing to close out the win. On the next line change, Hitchcock put enforcer Donald Brashear out, so Senators head coach Jacques Martin responded by positioning his enforcer Rob Ray beside Brashear. It did not take long for the two tough guys to find each other and go at it. Brashear got the better of Ray, cutting him above his left eye, and when the fight was over, both players were sent to their dressing rooms.

But before either of the enforcers could get off the ice, another Senators player went after Brashear, and then all the players on the ice went after each other, even goaltenders Senators Patrick Lalime and the Flyers Robert Esche. The referees ejected the offending players from the game, and order was gradually restored. On the ensuing faceoff, Sens coach Jacques Martin put out his other tough guy Chris Neil, and the moment the puck was dropped, Neil began pounding on forward Radovan Somik. That set off another line brawl, with Zdeno Chara dropping the gloves with Mattias Timander. At that point, Hitchcock was screaming at Martin for using his tough guys for a second time.

Calm was again restored, but once the puck dropped on the next faceoff, Mike Fisher of the Sens and Michael Handzus of the Flyers dropped their gloves, and John Leclair and Wade Redden paired off. Television announcers noticed that before the Leclair–Redden fight, Hitchcock had spoken to Handzus and Leclair and both players had shaken their heads in approval, most likely agreeing to fight on the next faceoff.

The linesmen tried to restore order, but both teams were determined to beat each other senseless. So many players were in the penalty box or in the dressing room that the Senators had just three players on the bench to play the rest of the game. When all was said and done and the final whistle blew, 20 players had been ejected from the game and it took officials about 90 minutes to sort out the penalties for each team. The Flyers ended up with 213 penalty minutes while the Senators received 206, for a combined record of 419 minutes.

After the game, in the corridors of the Flyers arena, Philadelphia general manager Bob Clarke had to be restrained from going after Sens head coach Jacques Martin.

"I understand Rob Ray fighting Donald Brashear. That's okay. Even Marck Recchi and Patrick Sharp, they can fight," said Clarke. "But don't go after guys who don't know how to defend themselves like Somik and Timander. What Neil did is not something to be proud of. I'm ticked off that a player like Neil would go after a player like Somik. If Martin says it's not his responsibility, then he doesn't have control of his bench."

The Flyers ended up winning the bout, 5–3.

Chapter 6

The Ugly Side of Hockey

Hockey is a man's game. The team with the most real men wins.

–Brian Burke

The McSorley Incident

Marty McSorley had a long career in the NHL as a fighter and was known to live strictly by the code. He was respected for it, and he still takes pride in following the code. He made a career with his fists, protecting such legends as Wayne Gretzky, but McSorley's career of incredible highs ended on an incredible low during a game in Vancouver in 2000.

By the 1999–2000 season, McSorley was in the twilight of his career. He had already accumulated over 3000 penalty minutes in his job of protecting the star players of the Edmonton Oilers. Fighting was his bread and butter, but McSorley was also a good defenseman and an integral part of two Stanley Cup championships with the Oilers in 1987 and '88. His name among enforcers was always one that was spoken with respect; he never fought dirty and knew that hockey in the end was just a job. Despite all those years in the league, it took only one incident in one game to change the history books on his hockey life.

On February 21, 2000, McSorley, then with the Boston Bruins, rolled into Vancouver for a battle against the Canucks. The main source of fireworks came from a meeting of McSorley and the Canucks heavyweight enforcer Donald Brashear. The two fighters had met on the battlefield several times over the years, and during the first shift of the game, they met on the ice to settle their score as the code of hockey generally dictates. In the fight, Brashear got the better of the veteran pugilist, getting in the most punches before tackling him to the ice. But what happened immediately afterward had McSorley fuming and out for blood.

As the linesmen jumped in to separate the two, Brashear took the opportunity to give McSorley one last shot to the face while he was down. Then when McSorley was in the penalty box, Brashear played it up to the raucous Canuck hometown crowd by dusting off his hands to embarrass McSorley, again violating the rules of the code. For the veteran McSorley, Brashear's gesture was a sign of disrespect. Once out of the box and back on the ice, McSorley did everything he could to invite Brashear to fight, but the Canucks forward would not bite.

Upset at being ignored, McSorley hit Brashear with a vicious cross-check to the kidneys. As McSorley sat in the penalty box for his 10-minute misconduct, Brashear took a few more liberties and parked himself in front of Bruins goaltender Bryon Dafoe. In the heat of the action, Brashear fell on Dafoe, injuring his knee and taking him out for the remainder of the season. McSorley sat in the penalty box, fuming mad. He knew that Brashear was purposely taking liberties, and as the code dictates, that Canuck had to answer to the Bruin's enforcer.

Late in the third period, Brashear skated by the Bruins bench and flexed his arm muscles, taunting the Bruins and showing further disrespect. With the game winding down, it fell to McSorley to right the wrongs Brashear had done to his team.

With just seconds left in the game (which the Canucks led 5–2), McSorley pursued Brashear through the neutral zone, trying to get him to answer for his misdeeds. Brashear ignored him, and according to the code, Brashear was acting the coward. With only two seconds left on the clock, McSorley's rage got the better of him, and he swung his stick at Brashear, hitting him squarely on the temple.

Brashear fell backward, instantly hitting the ice like a ton of bricks. His helmet flew off from the impact, and his unprotected head crashed into the concrete-like ice. Brashear lay motionless on the ice, and suddenly, his body began to seize. Fans gasped at the sight of Brashear twitching on the ice. Brashear was put on a stretcher and taken to hospital where doctors said he suffered a grand mal seizure and a severe concussion. Brashear ended up missing 20 games before returning to action.

For McSorley, his actions marked the end of his career. The NHL was quick to act and banned him from the league for one year—the longest suspension in league history at the time. Of course, with such a visual example of on-ice violence, the media coverage surrounding the incident blew up immediately and again sparked the predictable debate across North America every time a serious on-ice incident occurred.

Things got worse for McSorley when a British Columbia provincial court charged him with assault with a weapon and later found him guilty. He received an 18-month conditional discharge. McSorley sat out the remainder of the year and decided it was time for him to retire.

His decision was a sad end to a long and prestigious career, but many in the news media said that McSorley got what he deserved. But for the 17-year NHL veteran, the issue was not so black and white.

McSorley said in Ross Bernstein's 2006 book *The Code*, "A lot of people don't remember Donald standing in front of our bench, challenging and taunting us by flexing his muscles. You don't do that kind of Mickey Mouse garbage without backing it up in this league.... He had to be held accountable.... I certainly paid a high price for my actions and I accept that. That is something I will have to live with.... I am just sad that it happened the way it did and that it caused such a black eye for our sport. That was never my intention."

McSorley did not intend to injure Brashear to the degree he did, and he apologized for the outcome, but in the years since, McSorley has remained steadfast in his belief in the code, and that had his fellow enforcer adhered to it, like he did, then they would have had a fight and moved on. Brashear, however, chose not to see the hit in the same light and still considers it an assault.

The Bertuzzi Incident

In the history of the NHL, a few incidents have shaken the foundations of hockey. One of the most high-profile cases is the Todd Bertuzzi–Steve

Moore incident. This was not just another hockey play gone awry; the episode went to the very core of the infamous code of hockey and again divided even further those seeking change and those seeking the status quo. Basically, it boils down to those against the code and those for the code.

On February 16, 2004, the Vancouver Canucks met up to play the Colorado Avalanche in Denver. Both teams were well acquainted with each other, but not much of a rivalry had built up between them. That quickly changed.

Late in the game, the Canucks were nursing a 1–0 lead when Canucks captain Markus Naslund led his line up the ice on a rush. The puck got away from him in the neutral zone, and as he was stretching for the puck, Colorado forward Steve Moore swerved into him at high speed, striking him with his shoulder and arm. Naslund never saw the hit coming. He spun in the air and fell face first onto the ice, hitting his head and knocking him unconscious. Luckily for Naslund, his visor prevented him from also breaking his nose, but he still suffered a concussion, a jagged cut to his forehead and a hyperextended elbow.

The referees did not penalize Moore on the play, and a further review by the league disciplinary body agreed with the on-ice officials calling it a hockey play and an unfortunate incident. Legal hit or not, the Vancouver Canucks were livid. One of the most vocal on the subject was Canucks general manager Brian Burke. "Whether it's an elbow or not, it's clearly a head hunting shot on a star player by a marginal player," said Burke. "It's obvious the player dropped down to get him at head level. This was a chance to take out a star player and he took it."

Moore for his part claimed he was just trying to finish his check and had no ill intentions on the play. But the Canucks did not buy the excuses. The code of letting up when a player is dangerously exposed seemed long removed from the sport, and at the time, concussions to star players were becoming more common, and the league had yet to step in to protect those players.

"From the view that we had—and it was right in front of the bench—it looked like [Moore] knew what he was doing," said Canucks head coach Marc Crawford. "And it was a vicious hit, and a vicious hit against a star player should not be tolerated."

The most incendiary statement came from Canucks tough guy Brad May, who said after the game that there would be a bounty on Moore's head the next time the two teams faced off. Todd Bertuzzi also chimed in and said that Moore needed to be more careful out on the ice in the future.

To further incense the Canucks, their captain and league-leading scorer was expected to be out of action for up to two weeks. Luckily for the Canucks, Naslund made a speedy recovery and missed only three games. He was back in time for the rematch against Colorado on March 3, 2004. However, the league was watching both teams closely because of all the inflammatory language after the earlier game. Even NHL commissioner Gary Bettman and executive vice president Colin Campbell attended the game to make sure they were on hand to witness any infractions.

The NHL has always said that fighting is allowed in the sport, but premeditated or staged fights are strictly frowned upon. The game was played without much incident and ended in a 5–5 tie. There were, however, two fights—one between Canucks tough guy Wade Brookbank and Avs enforcer Peter Worrell and the other a minor skirmish between Bertuzzi and Avs defenseman Adam Foote. Steve Moore remained untouched the entire game.

With that game and the few fights, many thought that the teams had settled the score and moved on. Their next match-up, five days later on March 9, was expected by most people to be just another regular-season game, but the atmosphere turned from calm to tense when the Avalanche jumped to a 5–0 first-period lead. In between those goals, four fights erupted, including a tilt between Moore and Canucks tough guy Matt Cooke. The fight was not enough to satisfy the Canucks' code of honor, though, and throughout the game, Moore was constantly challenged to drop his gloves.

In the third period, with almost eight minutes left, Moore was again challenged by the Canucks minor-league call-up Sean Pronger. Moore simply turned away but was immediately confronted by Canucks forward Todd Bertuzzi. Keeping his back to Bertuzzi, Moore tried to skate away from the hulking forward, who kept tugging on Moore's jersey and inviting him to fight. Frustrated, Bertuzzi, still with his gloves on, suddenly swung and smacked Moore in the head from behind. The Avs forward was knocked unconscious by the right hook and collapsed face first onto the ice, followed by all of Bertuzzi's 240 pounds landing on his back.

The Avalanche players immediately rushed to Moore's defense, trying to pull Bertuzzi off him. The rest of the players on the ice paired off and started fighting, but when they realized that Moore was not moving, they made way for the trainers and focused their attention on their teammate. Even the crowd, which had been calling for blood a moment earlier, was now silent as the trainers examined Moore. A stretcher was brought out, and Moore's head and neck were immobilized before he was rushed out of the arena to a local hospital. He suffered a severe concussion and three fractured vertebrae in his neck.

After the game in the Canucks dressing room, the mood was decidedly somber, with all players apologizing and expressing deep regret over the incident. As a result of the media firestorm surrounding Bertuzzi, he faced the press the next day and fought back tears, offering an apology to Moore and all hockey fans. "Steve, I just want to apologize for what happened out there, that I had no intention of hurting you out there and that I feel awful for what transpired," he said. "To the fans of hockey and the fans of Vancouver, for the kids that watch this game, I'm truly sorry. I don't play the game that way. I'm not a meanspirited person. I'm sorry for what happened."

The NHL acted immediately, suspending the Vancouver forward for the rest of the season and the playoffs. The Vancouver Police Department also investigated and, months later, charged Bertuzzi with assault causing bodily harm, a charge he pleaded guilt to, receiving a conditional discharge with 20 hours of community service. He also lost about $500,000 in salary and about $350,000 in lost endorsement deals.

For 26-year-old Moore, the prognosis was much worse. Doctors told him that he would never again play hockey, and for a kid from Thornhill, Ontario, who was just starting out his career in the league, the news was devastating. Unable to play and suffering concussion symptoms years later, Moore filed a civil lawsuit in the province of Ontario in February 2006 against Bertuzzi, the Canucks and the parent company of the Canucks, Orca Bay Sports and Entertainment. Moore sought $15 million in damages for loss of income, $1 million for aggravated damages and $2 million for punitive damages.

NHL commissioner Gary Bettman did not like the bad press the lawsuit was bringing the league and tried to get Bertuzzi and Moore to settle out of court, but Bertuzzi's offer of $350,000 to settle the case was called an "insult" to Moore.

On March 28, 2008, Bertuzzi shocked many in the hockey world by filing a lawsuit against his former head coach at the time of the incident, Marc Crawford. The suit alleged that as a player, Bertuzzi was contractually obliged to obey Crawford, and therefore Crawford had to share in the responsibility of what happened that night. That lawsuit was dropped in January 2012, but the Moore v Bertuzzi case was set to go before the Ontario Superior Court in the fall of 2012.

For Moore, in the end, he just wants the NHL to wake up and see that something like this never occurs again. "The attack has been bad for our game," he said in a CBC interview. "I don't want to be the cause for any more negativity to the NHL. My biggest hope is that there's a serious evaluation of preventing this from happening again. There's been so much damage to the game. When you talk to people who don't know the game, the only thing you hear about is that it's so violent."

As for the code of hockey, it failed the players, the league and the fans in this case. Moore most likely felt he had answered the Canucks' revenge debt and did not need to fight once more, but the Canucks players and Bertuzzi obviously disagreed. In Bertuzzi's mind at the time, Moore was not playing the game by the code and needed to step up and fight. Bertuzzi, however, was the player in clear violation of the code. He attacked and sucker punched a player from behind and then added further insult to injury by slamming his head into the ground.

For others in the hockey world, had both parties followed the code, none of the violence would have occurred.

"The thing about the Bertuzzi incident that really bugged me was that he hit him from behind. I mean, if you want to sucker punch a guy, great, go for it, but do it to his face so he can see you," said Tony Twist in Ross Bernstein's book *The Code*. "But—and this is a big but—Moore was also at fault for running around and not turning to face him. He had it coming and he needed to take his medicine for the hit he dished out to Naslund. His fight with Cooke earlier on didn't really do much. He didn't answer the bell."

For former players like Tony Twist and a host of others, the role of the enforcer is to take incidents such as this and "teach" Moore a lesson for going after a team's star. Many people who think like Don Cherry would claim that the injury to Moore and other similar cases are in direct relation to the decline of the enforcer in the National Hockey League.

"I would have skated over to his bench and pointed right at him in front of his 19 teammates and said, 'When I get you out on the ice I am going to kick your ass, and just beat you for what you did.' That sends a very powerful message," said former tough guy and referee Paul Stewart, "and that kid would learn never to play that way again after a good ass whipping."

Twist, Cherry and Stewart claimed that hockey should govern itself. Many similar on-ice incidents had occurred prior to this one, but today, television cameras cover every game from every angle, able to replay and zoom in on the action to see violence in its most raw form. And with the advent of 24-hour sports networks and the Internet, these violent episodes put a negative spotlight on the game.

In the past, the NHL normally sided with the Cherrys and Stewarts of the game, but in the case of Moore, with the public pressure and the impeding lawsuits, the league was on his side. What swayed the NHL was its perception of the Bertuzzi incident as being revenge-based, and in such cases, the league will often side with the victim.

The NHL sells violence as part of the game, but violent revenge is the league's line in the sand. The NHL had long subscribed to the old Conn Smythe adage, "If you can't beat them in the alley, you can't beat them on the ice," but such incidents change the opinions, however slowly, of those behind the corporate desks, and as Moore would hope, maybe change the way the league deals with violence and the "code."

Comparing the McSorley and Bertuzzi Incidents

The common denominator of both the Todd Bertuzzi and Marty McSorley incidents is that they happened because the players did not follow the code of hockey. The problem is that the code is not a tangible thing, and each player acts according to his own personal set of rules. The definition of the code falls in a large gray area, and as a result, the debate on the best ways to prevent such on-ice incidents will continue to rage.

All the players and coaches involved in both the Bertuzzi and McSorley incidents were operating under the code of hockey. The McSorley–Brashear incident is a little easier to explain and judge when using the code of hockey. As for whether using the code at all in hockey is the right way to govern the game, that is a different matter.

On that night in February 2000, Marty McSorley was only doing his job—he was patrolling the ice and dropping the gloves against a fellow enforcer that he thought knew the unwritten rules of the game as he did. But when Brashear stepped over the line with his antics, and especially by injuring the goaltender, he was inviting trouble. That is clear enough. As an enforcer in professional hockey for several years at the time of the incident, Brashear should have been well aware of what the code required him to do, but he repeatedly refused to drop the gloves a second time with McSorley. The lack of respect for the unwritten rules of the game led directly to his injury, as unfortunate as it was. It truly was a regrettable action on McSorley's part, but it could have been avoided had Brashear stepped up and fought in the first place.

Todd Bertuzzi, on the other hand, completely disregarded the conventions of the code in 2004. In the immediate rematch after Steve Moore of the Colorado Avalanche injured Vancouver

Canucks Markus Naslund, several fights ensued that should have settled accounts. In the third meeting of the Avalanche and the Canucks, Moore eventually answered for his alleged crimes by fighting tough guy Matt Cooke. For the Canucks coach Marc Crawford and for Bertuzzi, that fight did nothing to satisfy the code of retribution.

No matter how quickly the fight between Moore and Cooke had ended, the rematch, plus the other earlier fights, should have been enough to settle the score between the teams. Crawford knowingly sent out Bertuzzi in the closing moments of a blowout loss to the Avalanche to seek the vengeance the Canucks wanted. The ultimate violation of the code came when Bertuzzi sucker punched Moore from behind. Every player knows that that action is just not acceptable in hockey.

The code of conduct in hockey and in the NHL has served the sport well over the years. At times it provides order in a physical and sometimes violent sport.

The Life and Death of Don Sanderson

Don Sanderson grew up in the 1990s, and like many Canadian kids, he dreamt of the day he could make a career playing in the NHL. When he was young, he showed early promise, scoring goals and skating like the wind. By the age of 16,

Sanderson was only a few years away from being a potential star with the NHL. In 2003, the Memorial Cup champion Kitchener Rangers drafted him. However, to the Rangers, Sanderson was more than just a goal-scoring phenom.

Sanderson's father, Mike, said in "The Code," a CBC *Fifth Estate* documentary, "The reason why they drafted him was his aggressiveness in hockey. Not saying that they were looking for him to fight because that was not his role, it was just his toughness, that he would go out and make the big hit and play physical along the boards and everything else."

After a few years playing with the Kitchener Rangers, it became clear to Sanderson that if he wanted a path to the NHL, it would not be the same as other players who move up through the juniors, get drafted and play in the NHL.

In his early 20s, playing hockey for York University, Sanderson was cut from the team, and for the first time in his hockey career, he was left without a team. With a continuing passion for the game, Sanderson found a spot with the Whitby Dunlops of the Ontario Hockey Association (OHA). The league was filled with players whose dreams of playing in the NHL were pretty much dead, but they still had something left to prove. Sanderson was not the most talented player on the ice, but he played with an intensity that won him the respect of his teammates. But to earn some of that respect, Sanderson had to drop his gloves from time to time.

"He didn't want to fight," said his father. "The only reason why he fought and got involved in it was because...he had to go to a teammate's aid."

Protecting your teammates at all costs is the unwritten rule of the game, and Don Sanderson was simply following it to the letter. He never hesitated or questioned going in to help a teammate because he did not want to be seen as a coward. Hockey ran through Sanderson's blood, and so did the code. However, Sanderson did not like fighting. He routinely called his father after games and told him that he had got into a fight, but that it was just part of the game. As the bigger guy on the ice, his job was to take care of problems when they arose.

In the OHA, players who fought were automatically thrown out of the game, but that did not stop Sanderson, who often told his father after a game that he had no choice when challenged. After his first fight of the 2008–09 season, Sanderson called his father and explained his reason for fighting.

"And he phoned me and goes, 'I got in a fight,' and I says, 'Why?' and he said 'Somebody went after our captain,' he says. 'You know what, my captain is a lot better and more important to the team and the guy dropped his gloves,' he says. 'What I am going to do, Dad? I got to defend myself.'"

Sanderson's response to his father was the code in action. If someone takes liberties with your star player, the bigger guy on the team has to defend the team's honor. This is the role of the enforcer, and like it or not, it's an integral part of the game.

During the 2008–09 season, Sanderson had already been in four fights despite the league rule of automatic ejection from the game. On the night of December 14, 2009, in a game against the Brantford Blast, Sanderson patrolled the ice as usual. He wasn't looking for trouble but was just out to play hard hockey. But as had happened in other games, Sanderson was called upon by the code of hockey to drop the gloves for his team. Fighting the Blasts Corey Fulton, another player known as a fighter, it started off like a normal hockey tussle—the tugging of jerseys, the throwing and dogging of punches—but when Sanderson's helmet was knocked to the ice in the skirmish, the fight suddenly took a turn for the worse.

After a few punches are thrown, both fighters will often wrestle and then fall to the ice before the linesmen separate them, but in this case, Sanderson's unprotected head hit the ice.

The other players immediately knew something was wrong when Sanderson didn't move. He regained consciousness briefly but eventually fell into a coma in the arena. The team trainers were called in, and Sanderson was rushed to hospital.

"The sight was just unbearable. Knowing that...I knew, right then and there, that my son probably died on the ice. It just wasn't fair," said Mike Sanderson about seeing his son in the hospital hooked up to life support. Twenty days later, on January 2, 2010, Don Sanderson died as a result of his injuries.

Following his death, there was a renewed attention to the role of fighting in hockey and the dangers that players face, even in the minor leagues. Radio stations were flooded with callers bitterly divided at what should or could be done about fighting in hockey. In the end, nothing was done, at all levels of hockey, and a family is left with only the memory of their son.

The Deaths of Bob Probert, Derek Boogaard, Rick Rypien and Wade Belak

At the time of this writing, no NHL player has ever died from a fight. However, with the recent deaths of four top enforcers in the league, this statement might need to be rephrased to say, "No NHL player has ever died from a single fight on the ice." But off the ice, fighting has been a factor in the deaths of several NHL players.

An enforcer wakes up in the morning knowing that he might have to drop his gloves. When he gets to the rink, he knows that his teammates are counting on him to fight. When the game starts, he knows the coach might lean over and give him that familiar tap on the shoulder. And when he goes to bed that night, he knows that he will have to do it all over again in the next game. For some players, the constant threat of physical violence builds up inside them and begins to eat away at their souls.

"Some guys I know couldn't sleep at night, sweat. I'd toss and turn at night. There's some nights I didn't get a good night's rest knowing what I needed to do the next night," said Nick Kypreos, former NHL tough guy whose career ended because of a severe concussion he sustained in a fight. "Knowing that inner battle that you have to do this job, but I've seen it torn guys apart, the inner battle between fighting and what it does to you and what it does for people around you; wives, children, parents. You know it's not a glamorous thing, and some guys really have trouble with it."

Bob Probert's career was the perfect example of that inner struggle some players experience. Despite having million-dollar contracts and

a beautiful life off the field, Probert battled drug
and alcohol abuse his entire career. Despite the
tough exterior of many of these players, several of
them struggle on the inside, and the culture
of hockey dictates that any such problems are
a sign of weakness and should be kept to themselves. As a result of the code of silence, players like
Boogaard and Probert turned to substance abuse to
quiet their inner demons. Most often the abuse is
in the form of prescription drugs, something that
is increasingly common in NHL locker rooms. The
Derek Boogaard story is the perfect example. Players know about the problems associated with the
proliferation of pain medications, sleep aids and
anxiety pills, but no one talks about it.

The solution to the problem of substance abuse
seems easy. Players need to talk about their problems and fears as they arise, but the culture of
hockey looks upon this frankness as weakness.
Hockey players are the toughest men in all of
sport, and they are expected to act that way. That
toughness is the hockey culture of Don Cherry,
a culture that has persisted since the NHL's formation.

You can almost hear the old hockey stories in
your head. Toronto Maple Leafs defenseman Bob
Baun scoring a Stanley Cup goal on a broken leg
but refusing to tell his trainers; Bobby Orr playing through incredible pain in the later stages of

his career because of repeated knee injuries; Maurice Richard sustaining a concussion and a black eye but still managing to score three goals in a game. These stories are engrained into the consciousness of every hockey player and every fan. They tell of a warrior-like attitude—win at all costs no matter the consequences. And the code is more important for the game's enforcers; they know their role and the pressure to live up to it is incredible.

Often the drug problems go hand in hand with severe depression, as was the case with Rick Rypien, Derek Boogaard and Wade Belak. All three players suffered from bouts of extreme depression that reduced these once-towering figures of strength to empty shells. It is an image that is hard to reconcile, and one that the NHL has been slow to react to, even with the recent deaths of several high-profile players. But while the league has not really moved on the issue of players' mental health and substance abuse, science has recently brought some interesting facts to light, specifically in the case of two of these players.

After the deaths of Derek Boogaard and Bob Probert, autopsies showed that both men had suffered from a degenerative brain disease called chronic traumatic encephalopathy (CTE). The disease is progressive and occurs in the brains of people who have had a history of head injuries, concussions or repeated blows to the head. Individuals with this disease show symptoms of dementia, memory loss, aggression, confusion and depression, all of which can appear within a few short months or decades after the head injuries have ceased. CTE fundamentally alters the physical makeup of the brain, including a reduction in the weight of the brain and a loss of neurons.

Since science has put a name to the medical condition, many players who have made or continue to make their livelihoods as enforcers are worried that they could have CTE or possibly develop the disease later in life. But the problem extends further, to the average player. Rick Martin, former member of the famed "French Connection" line with the Buffalo Sabres in the 1970s, died of a heart attack on March 13, 2011, at the age of 59. After his death, the autopsy revealed that he had suffered from CTE.

"Rick Martin's case shows us that even hockey players who don't engage in fighting are at risk for CTE, likely because of the repetitive brain trauma players receive throughout their careers," said Chris Nowinski of the Sports Legacy Institute.

The fact that a player who was not a fighter developed the disease is a striking example of the risks that all hockey players take during every game they play. If a player known as a scorer his entire career can develop CTE later in life, then the dangers a fighter faces is tenfold. While it is not publicly known whether Wade Belak and Rick Rypien suffered from CTE, the pressures of being an enforcer and the physical toll that position had on their bodies was a major contributing factor in their deaths.

Chapter 7

Tail of the Tape: Fighting Facts, Stats and Quotes

Four out of five dentists surveyed recommend playing hockey.

–Author unknown

Hockey has always been viewed as dangerous and violent, but statistically speaking, the game is a box of cute puppies in comparison to some other sports when it comes to the number of injuries. What qualifies a sport as the most dangerous can be measured and defined in a variety of ways. In the statistics that follow, the general approach was to look at the number of injuries per sport. Therefore, given these criteria, the sports with the highest number of injuries is the most violent.

Hockey violence has been chronicled heavily in the media, but the focus has been on specific violent incidents that bring negative attention to the sport. In the stats that follow, you will see that other sports have much higher incidents of injuries, which might make you think twice about hockey violence. The statistics are taken from the Advanced Physical Medicine website, using U.S. statistics.

The most common injuries for all the sports listed below are to the head (12 percent of all injuries), followed by ankle injuries and then finger injuries.

Top sports in terms of injuries by the numbers:

Sport	Ranking	Number of injuries
Basketball	1	2.56 million
Cycling	2	2.49 million
Football	3	2.38 million
Softball	4	1 million
Baseball	5	763 thousand
Skateboarding	6	676 thousand
Horseback riding	7	316 thousand
Golf	8	127 thousand
Ice hockey	9	105 thousand
Lacrosse	10	96 thousand

Most dangerous sports, with greatest number of injuries per number of participants:

Sport	Ranking	Number of injuries
Football	1	4.86%
Skateboarding	2	1.86%
Basketball	3	1.86%
Baseball	4	1.31%
Cycling	5	1.29%
Softball	6	1.11%
Ice hockey	7	0.57%
Volleyball	8	0.56%
Golf	9	0.18%
Tennis	10	0.14%

Based on the numbers, basketball and football appear to be the most dangerous sports. However, it is possible that the ice hockey stats would be higher in the rankings if more players reported injuries. Hockey is all about toughness and not showing weakness; for example, Bob Baun played in the 1964 Stanley Cup finals and did not tell anyone he had a broken leg.

NHL Penalty Records

Let Wayne Gretzky have the scoring records and Martin Brodeur take the shutout records. The guys listed in the following table will take the punching records.

Player	Games Played	Career	Career Penalty Minutes
Dave "Tiger" Williams	962	1974–88	3966
Dale Hunter	1047	1980–99	3565
Tie Domi	1020	1989–2006	3515
Marty McSorley	961	1983–2000	3381
Bob Probert	935	1985–2002	3300
Rob Ray	900	1989–2004	3207
Craig Berube	1054	1986–2003	3149
Tim Hunter	815	1981–97	3146
Chris Nilan*	688	1979–92	3043
Rick Tocchet	1144	1984–2002	2972

All-time penalty minutes leader, including playoffs: Dave "Tiger" Williams accumulated 4421 penalty minutes over his entire career. He was truly the master pugilist.

Single-season penalty record: Dave "The Hammer" Schultz, playing for the Philadelphia Flyers, accumulated an incredible 472 penalty minutes in 76 games during the 1974–75 season. That works out to an average of 6.21 minutes of penalties per game. Broad Street Bullies indeed. The second highest PIMs in a single season came at the fists of Paul Baxter in 1981–82, playing for the Pittsburgh Penguins.

Most penalties in one game: Chris Nilan accumulated an incredible 10 penalties in one game on March 31, 1991, when his Boston Bruins played the Hartford Whalers. The total included six minors, two majors, one misconduct and one game misconduct for a total of 42 minutes in one game.

Most penalty minutes in one game: Randy Holt started off his night playing for the Los Angeles Kings against the Philadelphia Flyers on March 11, 1979, with a simple two-minute penalty for holding, then three fighting majors, two 10-minute misconducts and three game misconducts, all totaling 67 minutes.

All-time playoff penalty record: Dale Hunter leads the pack with a record 729 penalty minutes in 186 playoff games. In second place is Chris Nilan with 541 penalty minutes in 111 playoff games.

Career penalty minutes record for goaltenders: Ron Hextall played in 608 career games and total 584 minutes in penalties. While many goaltenders stand by while the players duke it out, Hextall was never one to shy away from mixing it up, especially when a player got too close to his crease. He served several suspensions over his career, including an eight-game layoff for a vicious two-hand slash on the Edmonton Oilers Kent Nilsson and a 12-game suspension for his attack on the Canadiens Chris Chelios.

Billy Smith owns second place on the career penalty list with 489 PIMs in 680 games.

All-time playoff penalty record for goaltenders: Ron Hextall played in 93 playoff games and racked up 115 penalty minutes. Billy Smith racked up 89 minutes in penalties in 132 playoff games. Both goaltenders were known for their ability to clear players from their goal crease with impunity.

NHL record for most penalty minutes in one game: The Ottawa Senators and the Philadelphia Flyers (these two teams always seem to get involved in penalty records) hold this title with a total of 419 minutes. The world record for professional hockey though goes to Finland's top hockey league SM Liiga (Don Cherry squirmed when he heard this) in a game between Helsinki HIFK and Lahti Pelicans, after a line brawl cost both teams 465 minutes in penalties.

Although Dave "Tiger" Williams holds the record for most penalty minutes, the player to receive the most fighting majors in his career was Tie Domi. In all, the diminutive enforcer had 333 career fights. At five minutes per fighting major, that works out to 1665 minutes sitting in the penalty box.

Fighting Quotes

In Canada, you're not a hockey player until you lose some teeth.

–Andy Bathgate, former NHL player

I went to a fight the other night, and a hockey game broke out.

–comedian Rodney Dangerfield

We get nose jobs all the time in the NHL, and we don't even have to go to the hospital.

–Brad Park, former NHL player

A puck is a hard rubber disc that hockey players strike when they can't hit one another.

–Author unknown

I knew I was in trouble when I heard snap, crackle, and pop, and I wasn't having a bowl of cereal.

–Nick Kypreos, after hurting his ankle during a fight when playing for the New York Rangers

I wouldn't urinate in his ear if his brain was on fire.

–Bobby Hull, discussing a longtime rival

All my friends back home fight on the street, and they get arrested.

–Patrick Cote, enforcer for the Nashville Predators

If I play badly, I'll pick a fight in the third, just to get into a fight. I'll break a guy's leg to win, I don't care. Afterward I say, "Yeah, all right, I played badly, but I won the fight so who gives a damn."

–Bruin Derek Sanderson

I had a poster of [Bob] *Probert on my wall. When I fought him for the first and only time, I thought to myself, "Great, I got out alive."*

–Eric Cairns

Two people fighting is not violence in hockey. It might be in tennis or bowling, but it's not in hockey.

–former Bruins goaltender Gerry Cheevers

When I was playing in the American League, I went up to a guy in a game who speared me two years before that when I was playing university hockey. So, anyone else upstairs would say it's a staged fight. Well, it wasn't a staged fight.... And after the incident, he yelled at me, "What was that all about?" And I told him, I said, "You got me two years ago, and I didn't get a chance to get you for two years." It's not always a staged fight.

–Toronto Maple Leafs general manager Brian Burke

Without fighting, there would definitely be more stick work, some more cheap shots and cheap hits. Fighting keeps people accountable—they know there is the threat of a fight if things get too carried away.

–Calgary Flames forward Jarome Iginla

High sticking, tripping, slashing, spearing, charging, hooking, fighting, unsportsmanlike conduct, interference, roughing…everything else is just figure skating.

–Author unknown

Chapter 8

The Lighter Side of Fighting

Fighting is not all blood and guts. Sometimes even as men are punching each other there is time to learn something and laugh.

Rob Ray Rule

Rob Ray was a fighting specialist. You have to be to survive in the NHL for 900 career games playing the role of enforcer. You have to know your enemy, and you physically and mentally have to prepare yourself for every game. Ray had fighting down to a science.

Watch old footage of Ray before a fight, and you'll often see him remove his helmet, jersey and pads. He wasn't trying to show off his muscles—it gave his opponents nothing to grab onto in a fight. Trying to fight someone on skates is next to impossible because every time you throw a punch, you slide backwards. Ray knew this, and he would move in, grab onto his opponent's jersey and pound away at will. He became so successful with the tactic that NHL executives began to take notice.

It wasn't long before the league created a new rule that gave additional penalties to players who removed their jerseys or pads during a fight, and they required jerseys to be tied down with a strap. When the rule was implemented sometime in the 1990s, sportswriters dubbed it the "Rob Ray Rule," and Ray could not have been prouder.

> *When you think about it, it's all pretty amazing. I'm not the biggest guy in the world and I certainly didn't set out to be a fighter. When I was in the minors, I didn't think I could even do it on an every night basis, but I had a coach (John VanBoxmeer) who told me that if I wanted to get to this level I would have to be one of those guys who battled every night. I never thought I would have a rule named after me.*

Brave, But Stupid, Fan

On April 14, 1992, the Buffalo Sabres rolled into Le Colisee in Quebec City for an end-of-season tilt against the Nordiques. It was a horrible game for the visiting team, down 7–3 with just a few minutes on the clock. That was when a fan, naturally with a few beers in him, acted on a bet and jumped onto the ice and stupidly attacked the Sabres bench. His predicament was made even worse because he landed in front of the sixth most penalized player in NHL history—Rob "Rayzor" Ray. While other Sabres pulled on the fan's shirt, Ray unleashed a barrage of punches that all landed on the head of this poor stupid soul. Luckily for the fan, Quebec police were quick on their feet and saved him from further injury.

"It wasn't exactly self-defense," said Ray about the incident later, "after the first ten punches."

Montreal Canadiens forward Brian Skrudland commented on the one-sided fight, "All I know is that the guy on TSN said he landed 15 strong ones. Give the fan credit. He hung in there for 15 good ones, anyway."

When General Managers Fight

Conn Smythe, general manager of the Toronto Maple Leafs from 1927 to 1957, was well known for his fiery personality and stubborn work ethic. He was often at odds with players, and the people he worked with, and he had made more than a few enemies in his lifetime. But one general manager in particular raised Smythe's heart rate.

Boston Bruins general manager Art Ross never liked Smythe. Their two teams were bitter rivals, and each manager did whatever it took to get under the other's skin. When he played professional hockey, Ross was known for using every trick in the book to get an advantage over his competitors, a tactic that carried over to this management days. But Smythe was no slouch either.

Once, for no other reason than to enflame the passions of the Bruins' faithful and to raise the Ross' ire, Smythe took out a full-page ad in a Boston newspaper declaring, "Attention Hockey Fans! If you're tired of seeing the kind of hockey the Boston Bruins are playing, come to the Gardens (Boston Gardens) tonight, and see a real hockey club, the Toronto Maple Leafs!" Ross was not impressed.

However, Smythe was not the only person Art Ross did not get along with. Ross' habit of feuding with general managers began when he made the New York Americans general manager Red Dutton the target of his dislike. At an NHL Board of Governors meeting in 1936, Art Ross and Dutton actually traded blows.

During the meeting, the other GMs in attendance could see throughout the meeting that Ross had been purposely baiting Dutton for some unknown reason. The tension was building, so Detroit Red Wings general manager James Norris decided to do something before things got out of hand. Norris stepped in between the two men at the very moment that Ross whipped a punch at Dutton. Unfortunately, Norris' face got in the way. Furious at the attempted sucker punch, Dutton jumped on top of Ross and proceeded to beat him mercilessly until the fight was broken up. Ross left the meeting with a fractured nose and cheekbone and a few missing teeth—just like in the old days when he was a player.

The Gordie Howe Hat Trick

One of the most famous of milestones in hockey involves a player scoring a goal, getting an assist and getting into a fight. The namesake of the milestone, Gordie Howe, was well known throughout his career for his scoring prowess as well as his toughness. He did not get into many scraps, but when he did, Howe was usually the man ending them.

The first recorded "Gordie Howe hat trick" was achieved by the Toronto St. Pats Harry Cameron on December 22, 1920, long before Howe was born.

You might think Howe had several of these hat tricks during his six decades in professional hockey, but "Mr. Hockey" achieved just two.

His first Howe hat trick came on October 11, 1953, when Howe fought Toronto Maple Leafs Fern Flaman, assisted on a Red Kelly goal and scored his own. His second hat trick occurred in that same season, playing against the same team—the Toronto Maple Leafs. On March 21, 1954, he scored the opening goal of the game, assisted on two goals and fought Leafs legend Ted Kennedy.

One of the most amazing facts about the Gordie Howe hat trick is that on November 14, 1992, in a game between the Buffalo Sabres and the New York Islanders, three separate players achieved the feat. Tom Fitzgerald and Benoit Hogue of the Islanders and Wayne Presley of the Sabres all achieved the unique milestone. On April 5, 2012, Joe Thorton and Ryane Clowe of the San Jose Sharks each recorded a Howe hat trick in a game against the Los Angeles Kings.

In the history of recording this unusual statistic, Stan Mikita holds the record for the most Gordie Howe hat tricks (22) in his NHL career that spanned 22 years. Gordie Howe's one-time teammate Ted Lindsay comes in at second place with 19 Howe hat tricks in his career, while Brendan Shanahan rounds out third place with 17.

Maybe the name should be changed to the "Stan Mikita hat trick" since Gordie Howe achieved the feat just twice.

The Battle of the Hockey Enforcers

Imagine an event that stripped away the goals, the skill, the goaltenders, the coaches and the rules and left only hulking enforcers pounding each other in the face solely for the purpose of entertainment in a boxing type of format.

It was called Battle of the Hockey Enforcers, and on August 29, 2005, a crowd of 2000 people gathered to watch large men pound away at each other for a grand prize of $62,000.

Promoted by entrepreneur Darryl Wolski, the event was criticized heavily for reducing hockey to its complete and utter lowest common denominator. At first, no community wanted to host such an event, but eventually the city of Prince George, British Columbia, agreed—under the condition that helmets remained on at all times. Apart from that, the rules for the battle were simple: no fighting was allowed if they fell to the ice, and if the fight turned too one-sided, the referee could stop the fight.

The most famous participant in the event was former NHL enforcer Link Gaetz, "The Missing Link," with the rest of the fight card filled up with career minor leaguers and non-hockey tough guys who could barely stand on skates. The event began with 16 fighters and ended with Dean Mayrand winning the final bout over Mike

Sgroi. Link Gaetz was taken out of the competition in the first round after getting knocked down twice. He later complained of concussion-like symptoms.

Rock 'Em, Sock 'Em Hockey

Don Cherry's philosophy of hockey can be summed up simply by watching any one of his (to date) 22 *Rock 'Em, Sock 'Em Hockey* videos that feature a compilation of NHL highlight goals, plays, saves, bloopers, hits and fights throughout the regular season and during the Stanley Cup playoffs, all colorfully and gleefully narrated by Don Cherry and often backed by terrible techno or rock music.

The first video was released in 1989 before the advent of the Internet and was an immediate success. To date, the franchise, which is produced by his son's company, Tim Cherry Enterprises, has sold over two million copies, and if you have never received one for Christmas, then you are not a real hockey fan.

If you want to have a good laugh, I suggest finding *Rock 'Em, Sock 'Em 5* and have a listen to Don Cherry trying his hand at rap (yes, Don Cherry hip-hop!). It starts off like this, "Probert, Probert, what a man! When you see him it's Wham Bam!"

Yes, it's that good.

Defense Mechanism

During a particularly rough hockey pre-season game in 1958, New York Rangers forward Camille Henry, one of the smallest players in the league at the time, lost his temper and found himself toe-to-toe with one of the game's most feared tough guys, a rugged defenseman from the Boston Bruins named Fernie Flaman, who outweighed Henry by some 75 pounds. As they grappled, gripped and grabbed, angling for advantage, pint-sized Henry suddenly shouted a warning to Flaman. "Watch out Fernie," Henry screamed over the roar of the crowd, "or I'll bleed all over you!"

When Brothers Fight

Charlie Conacher was the first NHLer to fight his brother, Lionel, in the 1930s. Since that fight, no other brothers have ever dropped the gloves until Hartford's Keith Primeau went toe-to-toe against his younger brother, Wayne, of the Buffalo Sabres in 1996–97.

Brothers fight all the time, so it's surprising that it is such a rare occurrence in the NHL, considering many brothers have played in the league at the same time. You'd figure one of the Sutters would have dropped them at one point, given that six brothers (Brent, Brian, Darryl, Duane, Rich and Ron) all played in the NHL against each other.

When Wayne and Keith Primeau joined the NHL, both played tough physical hockey, but neither believed they would ever fight against the other. They were family, after all. That is, until April 7, 1997, when their two clubs met. In the course of the game when the two were on the ice and the Sabres were in the Whalers zone, Wayne began making a nuisance of himself in front of goaltender Sean Burke. Keith came in and gave Wayne a hard cross-check that set off a scuffle.

As the two siblings stood up holding onto each other's jerseys, Keith asked his brother, "What do you want to do?" to which Wayne replied, "Whatever." The two went at it, though neither of them really gave it their all. The fight ended when Wayne fell to the ice and the linesmen stepped in. Wayne later spoke about fight with his brother. "We were a little disappointed in what we did," he said. "But we also knew it was part of the game, and it had to happen when it did. My dad was laughing, but she (mother) was pretty upset. She didn't want to see that happen again."

Foreign Object on the Ice

Early in his career, Bobby Hull was known for two things: his amazing talent and his golden hair that flowed majestically as he sped down the ice to score one of his many goals. With his chiseled good looks, the "Golden Jet," poster boy for the

NHL was extremely sensitive about his hair, especially when it started to fall out. Unable to accept losing his hair, Hull became the first known player in professional hockey to wear a toupee.

In the late 1970s, Hull played with the World Hockey Association, and every player knew that he wore a hairpiece, but no one was foolish enough to mess with the Golden One's new do. After all, not only was Hull a good scorer, but he could also fight with the best of 'em. He was never one to shy away from a fight, even with an expensive rug on his head.

Despite the threat of taking a beating, Dave Hanson, famous for the role he played in the movie *Slapshot*, was curious enough to attempt a hair removal. On April 14, 1978, Hanson's Birmingham Bulls were up against Hull's Winnipeg Jets in a tense playoff series. When a scuffle broke out in the corner of the rink, Hull and Hanson were right in the thick of the action. While Hull was distracted in the pile, Hanson snuck in behind the hockey legend and ripped off the toupee. However, as said by Frank Mahovlich, who happened to be in the arena that night, Hanson did more than just remove his hair.

"He jumped up behind Bobby Hull and pulled Hull's wig off," said Mahovlich, who watched in disbelief. "And in those days, the wigs were sewn in, they were stitched into your head. And Bobby started to bleed from the top down, and the blood was coming all over and he had to walk off the ice. It was an embarrassment in a lot of ways. That was one of the stories that happened. It wasn't a pleasant thing. It happened so quick. I don't know what he was doing, he just did it."

Too embarrassed to pursue his exposer or his hairpiece, which lay on the ice, Hull rushed to the dressing room for repairs and returned to action wearing a helmet and several shades of red on his face.

Chapter 9

Final Words

Fighting in hockey is a divisive topic. The debate about whether it should remain in the game rages on through all levels, dividing people down ideological lines. It is not an easy question to answer.

Enforcers like Eddie Shore, Sprague Cleghorn, Dave Schultz and Bob Probert, among others, have all made their mark on the game and its history. The game we watch today would definitely be less without them. They are the type of players who make the big hits and get us up on our feet. They are also the players who unite their teams and push them to greater glory. I cannot imagine an NHL without a Bob Probert or a Tie Domi.

Understand also the nature of the beast that is the NHL. The athletes are competitive players, everyone wearing a jersey wants to win the

Stanley Cup and most will do anything to achieve that goal. If getting into a fight will bring that goal closer, then more's the better. At the visceral level, for anyone who has played hockey, sometimes you get pissed off by a player constantly hacking at your ankles or a well-timed face wash, making fights inevitable. The league has to regulate that, of course, and it has. The question that remains, though, is how effective are they at getting the job done?

As much as I look back with fondness on the league and the pugilists that have populated my memories of the game, I can also remember the Canada Cups, the Olympic tournaments, the 1972 Summit Series; all amazing displays of hockey skill, minus the constant threat of violence. Can you imagine a league where Mario Lemieux and Wayne Gretzky could rule the ice, unimpeded, displaying the skill and potential of the game and what it could be without fighting?

The reality is that hockey has changed. The players are bigger, the game is faster and the stakes are higher. The days of the Original Six are long gone. The code might have served the players well in a small six-team league where guys had to respect one another. The modern NHL seems to have lost that respect. Look to the Matt Cooke hit on Marc Savard, the Mike Richards hit on David Booth or the Zdeno Chara hit on Max

Pacioretty, plays that received little or no suspensions from the league and in some cases even less understanding of the effects of their actions.

Hockey is a dangerous sport, played on a razor's edge between life and death. This was something that was understood in the Original Six years, and the level of fighting and violence was kept in check. And the debate is not just about media attention—we have just gotten smarter. We know more now about the effects physical violence is having on the players. The tragic examples of Wade Belak, Bob Probert, Rick Rypien and Derek Boogaard are a warning sign that hockey must acknowledge. The memories, health and the safety of future players must be honored and protected.

What then is the solution? Fighting will always exist in hockey. But facts cannot be ignored for the sake of nostalgia. Players' lives are at risk, and their health is not something to be toyed with because of a longing for the good ole days. The solution, though, is not an easy one. It's tough to accept, but people love violence, and violence sells tickets. Without those sales, Crosby or Gretzky would not have had jobs. Change has to be implemented, but slowly.

The league could increase fines to players who fight—one fight and you're out of the game; another fight, you're suspended; another fight and you're out for a long suspension; another fight and you're out for the season. The NHL needs to show leadership, and it will trickle down through the league. If the enforcer is no longer feared, then the league must become the enforcer. Only then will fighting be reduced, violence brought to a minimum and respect brought back to the game.

The question is: Does anybody want that change to happen?

Fighting in Hockey: A Timeline

1800s: Hockey is born on the frozen ponds and lakes of Nova Scotia. Although no record of any fights exists, you can almost be certain that a fight had to have broken out over a disputed goal, a slash to the hands or a bet not honored.

1875: On March 3, at the Victoria Skating rink in Montreal, two teams played in the first recorded indoor hockey game. As reported by the *Montreal Gazette* at the time, the game provided much excitement as the players "wheeled and dodged each other," and "the spectators then adjourned well satisfied with the evening's entertainment." The game went off without a problem, but it was after the game was over that a fight broke out between the hockey players and members of the Skating Club who were opposed to the hockey players damaging their ice. Voice were raised, insults were thrown about, and according to the

Kingston newspaper, *Daily British Whig*, "Shins and heads were battered, benches smashed and the lady spectators fled in confusion."

1922: NHL introduced Rule 56 to regulate fighting. The rule stated that players who engaged in "fisticuffs," as it was called in the rulebook, were to be given a five-minute major penalty.

1925: In order to open up hockey to American markets, owners of teams such as the Boston Bruins and the New York Rangers use fighting to market the game to a new audience.

1927: Boston Bruins Billy Coutu starts a bench-clearing brawl in game four of the 1927 Stanley Cup finals against the Ottawa Senators. The story goes that he started the brawl at the request of his coach Art Ross, by punching one referee and tackling another. Both benches cleared, and a brawl ensued. For his actions, Coutu was expelled from the NHL for life by NHL president Frank Calder.

1933: In a game between the Toronto Maple Leafs and the Boston Bruins, Bruins defenseman Eddie Shore is knocked to the ice by Leafs player King Clancy. Shore, believing it was Leafs forward Ace Bailey who had delivered the hit, seeks his revenge and knocks Bailey to the ice nearly killing the Leafs star player. Bailey recovered but never played hockey again.

1955: After an on-ice brawl in which he punched a eferee, Montreal Canadiens superstar Maurice "Rocket" Richard is suspended for the remainder of the season and the playoffs by league president Clarence Campbell. On the night of March 17, 1955, a Montreal hockey fan sets off a smoke bomb in the Montreal Forum during a game between the Canadiens and the Detroit Red Wings, touching off what has become known as "The Richard Riot."

1969: On September 21, Wayne Maki and the Boston Bruins "Terrible" Ted Green are involved in a stick-swinging incident that resulted in Green suffering a fractured skull that nearly killed him and effectively ended his career. Although Green suffered the worst injury, both players were charged with assault. This was the first time in the history of the NHL that a player was charged for an incident that occurred during a game.

1971: NHL creates the "third man in" rule in order to cut down on bench-clearing brawls. The rule stated that the first player to join a fight already in progress is ejected from the game.

Early 1970s: The "Big Bad" Bruins and the Broad Street Bully Philadelphia Flyers rise to the top of the league, using intimidation and fighting to both win two Stanley Cups by 1975.

1980s: Era of the Enforcer. Dave Semenko and Marty McSorley of the Edmonton Oilers are the poster boy policemen of the league watching over the Great One, Wayne Gretzky.

April 20, 1984: In game six of the second round series between the Montreal Canadiens and the Quebec Nordiques, the teams were involved in what came to be known as the "Good Friday Massacre." In total, two brawls broke out, Canadiens forward Jean Hamel was sucker punched in the eye knocking him unconscious (the injury ended his career), 10 players were ejected and 252 penalty minutes were handed out. The Canadiens won the game 5–3 and took the series.

January 4, 1987: The "Punch-up in Piestany", was the bench-clearing brawl between Canada and the Soviet Union during the World Junior Ice Hockey Championships. The brawl was so out of control that officials turned off the arena lights in an effort to stop the fighting.

1992: The NHL installs the "Instigator Rule" that states that the player starting a fight is given an additional two-minute minor penalty.

February 21, 2000: Marty McSorley of the Boston Bruins swings his stick and hits Vancouver Canucks Donald Brashear in the head, causing Brashear to fall backwards and hit his head on the ice. McSorley claims he was just trying to instigate a fight with Brashear. For the assault, McSorley was given 18 months probation and would never play in the NHL again.

March 3, 2004: Todd Bertuzzi of the Vancouver Canucks sucker punches forward Steve Moore of the Colorado Avalanche, knocking Moore out cold and fracturing his neck in the fall to the ice. The attack was revenge for a hit Moore had delivered on the Canucks captain Markus Naslund in a previous game. Moore has not played a game of hockey since.

March 5, 2004: In a game between the Philadelphia Flyers and the Ottawa Senators, five consecutive brawls break out during the final minutes of the third period. In all, 419 minutes in penalties were handed out—an NHL record.

December 12, 2008: Don Sanderson, of the minor league Whitby Dunlops, is involved in a fight with a player from the Brantford Blast. Sanderson is rushed to hospital after falling and hitting his head during the fight. He fell into a coma and died three weeks later.

July 5, 2010: Famed enforcer Bob Probert dies suddenly of a suspected heart attack. It was later announced that Probert suffered from chronic traumatic encephalopathy (CTE), a degenerative brain disease caused by repeated blows to the head.

May 13, 2011: NHL super tough guy Derek Boogaard dies from an accidental drug and alcohol overdose while recovering from a concussion. Autopsy revealed that he was suffering from the same condition as Probert—CTE.

August 15, 2011: NHL tough guy Rick Rypien commits suicide after a lifelong battle with clinical depression.

August 31, 2011: Wade Belak is found dead in his home of an apparent suicide, after suffering for several years with clinical depression.

List of Fighting Terms

"Wanna go?": What one player says to another player when he wants to fight.

Brouhaha: Another term used to describe a fight.

Cheap shot: A punch thrown when the intended target is not prepared or unable to defend himself.

Chirp: When two players insult each other, usually to goad the other into a fight or penalty.

Dropping the gloves: When two players throw off their hockey gloves to fight. Keeping them on would risk injury to their hands.

Enforcer: A player who is quick to fight and defend or protect his teammates when necessary.

Fight strap: The strap inside the back of a player's jersey that hooks into the pants, so that the jersey cannot be pulled over a player's head during a fight.

Fisticuffs: Old word for a fight.

Goon: A hockey tough guy who does not respect the rules of the code and is out to cause trouble and hurt players on the ice.

Intimidation: A tactic used by fighters to deter players from taking liberties on the ice.

Knuckle sandwich: A punch to the mouth.

Line brawl: A series of fights involving all the players on the ice fighting at the same time.

Pecking order: The hierarchy that governs the world of the hockey enforcer. The veterans are normally considered to be at the top while rookies must work their way up the "pecking order."

Penalty box ("The Sin Bin"): The area off ice where a penalized player must sit for a designated amount of time.

Pugilist: A term taken from the boxing world, meaning a fighter.

Scrap: Another term for a fight.

Scuffle: When two players drop the gloves but do not throw any punches.

Sucker punch: A punch to a player who is turned away from his aggressor.

Throwing down the gauntlet: When two players drop their gloves to fight.

Notes on Sources

Print Sources

Allen, Kevin, and Bob Duff. *Without Fear: Hockey's 50 Greatest Goaltenders*. Chicago: Triumph Books, 2002.

Allen, Kevin. *Crunch: Big Hitters, Shot Blockers and Bone Crushers. A History of Fighting in the NHL*. Chicago: Triumph books, 1999.

Bernstein, Ross. *The Code*. Chicago: Triumph Books, 2006.

Best, Dave. *Canada Our Century in Sport: 1900–2000*. Markham: Fitzhenry and Whiteside, 2002.

Diamond, Dan, and Eric Zweig. *Hockey's Glory Days: The 1950s and '60s*. Kansas City: Andrews McMeel Publishing, 2003.

Diamond, Dan, ed. *Total NHL.* Toronto: Dan Diamond and Associates, 2003.

McDonnell, Chris. *Hockey's Greatest Stars: Legends and Young Lions.* Willowdale: Firefly Books, 1999.

Podnieks, Andrew, et al. *Kings of the Ice: A History of World Hockey.* Richmond Hill: NDE Publishing, 2002.

Probert, Bob, and Kirstie McLellan Day. *Tough Guy: My Life on the Edge.* Toronto: Harper Collins, 2010.

Proteau, Adam. *Fighting the Good Fight: Why On-ice Violence Is Killing Hockey.* Toronto: Wiley Press, 2011.

Web Sources

ca.sports.yahoo.com/nhl/blog/puck_daddy/post/The-10-best-player-inspired-NHL-rules-changes?urn=nhl,263622

en.wikipedia.org/wiki/Tiger_Williams

hockeystoughguys.blogspot.ca/2006/08/bob-probert.html

oilersnation.com/2012/4/1/april-fools-2

sportsillustrated.cnn.com/hockey/nhl/news/2001/03/29/leafs_flyers_ap/

sportsillustrated.cnn.com/vault/article/maga-
zine/MAG1004135/1/index.htm

www.advancedphysicalmedicine.org

www.cbc.ca/sports/story/2004/02/27/Hav-
lat0228.html

www.cbc.ca/sports/story/2004/03/07/clarke
030407.html

www.habseyesontheprize.com/2009/8/18/
994087/bakers-dozen-of-strange-and

www.nytimes.com/2011/12/06/sports/hockey/
derek-boogaard-a-brain-going-bad.html?
pagewanted=1&_r=2&hp

www.prohockeyfights.com/forums/viewtopic.
php?p=37&sid=e0e83f44ffd1b3d49f2fdcecda23
dffa

www.torontosun.com/2011/09/02/ex-tough-
guys-divided-on-fighting

www.torontosun.com/2011/09/08/nilan-the-
fight-of-his-life

www.usatoday.com/sports/hockey/games/
2004-03-06-philly-ottawa_x.htm

www.youtube.com/watch?v=dh_uLi6Bf7s

www.youtube.com/watch?v=IbTAYukpv8I

J. Alexander Poulton is a writer, photographer and genuine enthusiast of Canada's national pastime. A resident of Montreal all his life, he has developed a healthy passion for hockey ever since he saw his first Montreal Canadiens game. His favorite memory was meeting the legendary gentleman hockey player Jean Beliveau, who in 1988 towered over the young awe-struck author.

He earned his B.A in English Literature from McGill University and his graduate diploma in Journalism from Concordia University. He has more than 25 books to his credit, including *Canadian Hockey Record Breakers, Greatest Moments in Canadian Hockey, Greatest Games of the Stanley Cup, Canadian Hockey Trivia, Hockey's Hottest Defensemen, The Montréal Canadiens, The Toronto Maple Leafs, Sidney Crosby, Does This Make Me Look Fat? Canadian Sport Humour* and *A History of Hockey in Canada,*

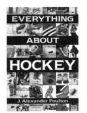
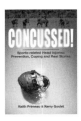

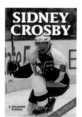

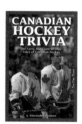